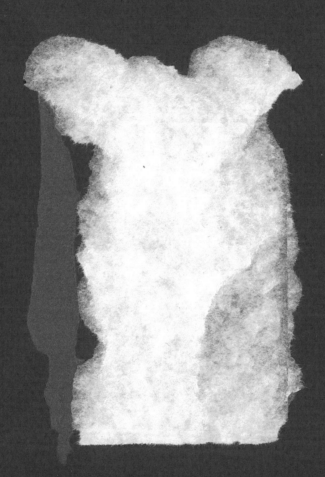

The Steps of Bonhoeffer

The Steps of

Bonhoeffer

a pictorial album

J. Martin Bailey / Douglas Gilbert

Pilgrim Press :: Philadelphia :: Boston

The publisher wishes to express appreciation to the individuals and publishers who granted permission to quote copyrighted materials. A list of acknowledgments is given on pages 127-28.

The photographs in this volume follow, as closely as possible, the Chronology of Events and Places on pages 18–22. The quotations selected from the writings of Dietrich Bonhoeffer generally are from a somewhat later period, many having been found among reflections written while he was imprisoned at Tegel.

The poem "Stations on the Road to Freedom," stanzas of which are used to introduce the sections of this book, was written on the evening of July 21, 1944, the day after the unsuccessful attempt to assassinate Adolf Hitler. Bonhoeffer's close friend and biographer, Eberhard Bethge, believes that by that time Dietrich was convinced the end of his personal and national hopes was close at hand.

For those who found freedom
with Dietrich Bonhoeffer

*He stands for all in our time who act according to their con-
science, who go against the stream, who will not submit to
wrong.*

—Ronald Gregor Smith

Foreword

Not only in Germany but all over the world, people are reflecting on the life and message of Dietrich Bonhoeffer. There is nothing self-evident about this. So many valuable men and women lost their lives in 1945; and Bonhoeffer was a young man who was only just beginning his real life-work, as measured by human standards. He had collected his first ecumenical experience and was regarded by the comparatively small circle of people who knew him as a man of whom much might be expected but who had not yet had an opportunity of exercising a wider influence. When we heard of his death we said to each other what a profound tragedy it was that Bonhoeffer was taken from us before he had any opportunity to make his personal contribution to the ecumenical movement.

We were wrong. He has made that contribution all the same. Hardly any man of his generation has more influence than he on the Christian church today. Both within the churches and outside them, among theologians and among the laity, he receives as much attention as if he were still living and writing. His ideas are used, exploited, and sometimes misapplied. A whole literature already exists commenting on Bonhoeffer, in many languages. A few days ago my friend D. T. Niles sent me a book, which he wrote in his own country of Ceylon and had published in America, in which he replies to the interpretation placed on Bonhoeffer by the Bishop of

Woolwich, J. A. T. Robinson, by giving an excellent analysis of Bonhoeffer's last letters. Bonhoeffer evokes a response all over the world and speaks to us as if he were still among us. Involuntarily we are reminded of another man who also lived to be 39 years old—Blaise Pascal. In both cases their lives were short, but they were like meteors in their dazzling intensity. In both cases their lives were cut off prematurely, but that is just what makes them so infinitely important for us. It is just because they are incomplete that Pascal's *Pensées* and Bonhoeffer's *Ethik* and letters compel us to share in their thinking and to carry it a stage farther. Like Socrates, their task was like that of a midwife, the task of raising the fundamental question. And they did raise it in its most crucial form: "What does it really mean to live in the world with Christ?" Their message to us is that life is too short to be lived half-heartedly.

From beginning to end Dietrich Bonhoeffer is concerned with making Christianity a reality in the world. In his first address as Youth Secretary of the World Alliance for Promoting International Friendship Through the Churches, given in 1932, he said that the gospel and the Law must be applied to the concrete situation, because the church is Christ present today. And during the last years when he was working on his *Ethics*, he opposed every attempt to separate Christ and the world in such a way that there was never any real confrontation between them. It is

wrong to separate the penultimate from the ultimate, time from eternity, creation from redemption, so that there is no longer any connection. Seen in the light of the divine incarnation, Christian life means participating in Christ's encounter with the world.

Is not this hunger and thirst for reality, for becoming incarnate, for *living* the Christian life and not merely *talking* about it the real key to Bonhoeffer's message? In my view both his writings and his life form an impressive unity, because his concern always remains this same thing. His warning against cheap grace in discipleship is closely connected with his opposition to "the religious," i.e., to fixing God in forms which are incomprehensible to the world today and which have no relevance for it. In the great, vital decisions which he takes we see even more clearly how he fights for the living God—not for a God who is absent, but for the God who wants to live in Christ among men, and who shows them a new way and leads them toward it.

The first decision was his decision for the Confessing Church. From the very outset Bonhoeffer had insisted that the church does not exist in order to proclaim eternal truths or principles, but in order to tell men what God's message is here and now in the most concrete way. Even before the church struggle, addressing an ecumenical youth conference in Czechoslovakia in 1932, he said, "The church is Christ's presence on earth. That is the only reason why its word has authority. . . . As the word which springs from Christ present within it, the word of the church must be a word that is valid and binding here and now." And now the hour had struck when the Christians in Germany had to say definitely whether they wanted to belong to a church like that, and not to a church that wanted to withdraw from the contemporary scene, nor to a church that was a syncretistic mixture of the Word of God and of pagan ideology. For Bonhoeffer it was certainly a liberation that he could now fight for a church which had a definite face. Had it not been for the events of 1933 (he said) he might have become a professor at one of the big theological faculties. "But the present situation permits me to do something far better, namely, to seize all the opportunities of direct expression in a persecuted church."

To Bonhoeffer the Confessing Church was not some special school of theology or ecclesiastical party. He went so far as to say, "Anyone who deliberately dissociates himself from the Confessing Church cuts himself off from salvation." At that hour the Confessing Church was simply the church of Christ. That must be said to everyone, not only in Germany, but also in the ecumenical movement where some people still regarded the church struggle merely as one of the usual theological conflicts that can only be ascribed to *rabies theologorum*.

From 1933 to 1935 Bonhoeffer was a pastor in London. There he had an important task, for he was the liaison-officer between the Confessing Church and Bishop Bell of Chichester. He could therefore feel that he was serving the good cause. However, he came to the conclusion that he must return to Germany in response to Karl Barth's call, "Back with one of the very next boats, back to the country where the church is in flames." Bonhoeffer had to abandon his dream of going out to India for a time. Instead of that he went to the illegal seminary in Finkenwalde and took up his position in the danger-zone.

His second decision was the decision for the ecumenical movement. It is not easy today to understand that the ecumenical cause can involve danger, and that maintaining solidarity with Christians all over the world can lead to open conflict with the state authorities. Today, unfortunately, we take the ecumenical movement more or less for granted. But at the time when Bonhoeffer was active things were different. It was in 1931 that his real ecumenical work began. But already in 1933 the government of the church in Germany passed into the hands of men who either tried to reconcile the church with National-Socialism, or at any rate did everything possible to keep on good terms with those in power. And the attitude of the national-socialists was quite clear. They regarded the ecumenical movement as a form of decadent liberal internationalism, and as a negation of nationhood (which they considered as the sole absolute value).

The ecumenical movement was still young, and only very few people had realized that it was not a Christian edition of the international movement, but a new form of the universal church born of the nature of the universal lordship of Christ. Bonhoeffer had already realized this. In 1932, when he was only twenty-six, he stood up at an ecumenical conference and protested against the superficiality of the ecumenical organizations. "They have no anchorage in theology to enable them to withstand the waves surging all around them." The ecumenical movement must be the expression of a very definite concept of the church, namely, that "the church, as the congregation of the Lord Jesus Christ, who is Lord of the world, has the task of giving its message to the whole world." The ecumenical movement therefore did not exist merely in order to promote ecumenical friendship, practical cooperation, or theological understanding. Its real raison d'être was joint proclamation of the Word of God—concrete, living, and renewing.

Two years later, in 1934, at its meeting in Fanö (Denmark), came the crucial hour for the ecumenical movement. The church struggle in Germany had begun. Should the ecumenical movement take a definite attitude toward it? "No," said many clever, cautious churchmen outside Germany, "we should not interfere in the internal problems of Germany." "No," said the "German Christians," of course, and also the people in the "center" of the church. But a few men, led by Bishop Bell of Chichester, who had learned a great deal from his conversations with Bonhoeffer, realized that if the ecumenical movement did not say or do anything at that moment it would be abandoning its own deepest concern. If it did not concern the ecumenical movement that a hard struggle was going on in Germany for the purity and the truth of the Christian message, then no real church-fellowship existed, no Christian solidarity, no mutual sharing of responsibility and suffering. The meeting at Fanö took a definite stand about the church struggle. That was a decision of tremendous importance for the whole future history of the ecumenical movement. And to a large extent it was due to Bonhoeffer, especially through his influence on Bishop Bell. So he also had the right to write his sharp paper on "The Confessing Church and the Oikoumene," in which he told the ecumenical movement that no one would believe in it if it did not give its unequivocal support to the Confessing Church, and in which he also told the Confessing Church that it must clearly state its close sympathy with the ecumenical movement, even if it were difficult and dangerous to do so.

Bonhoeffer acted in accordance with this conviction. He did everything possible in order to maintain the contacts that he had with so many churches, especially during the war years. In this way he definitely helped those churches never to forget their deep fellowship with the Confessing Church in Germany.

The third decision was certainly the most difficult of all. It was the decision to take up active political resistance to National-Socialism and to cooperate in a coup d'etat. Was it really necessary for Bonhoeffer to take this decision? He could easily have said that his task lay in an entirely different sphere. Of course, everything spoke against a Lutheran theologian taking up the struggle against his "authorities" and even cooperating in a plot to get rid of those "authorities" by force. Everything in Bonhoeffer's own life really spoke against it too. He had always struggled for peace. He had been so impressed by Mahatma Gandhi's use of nonresistance to achieve political ends that he had seriously thought of going to live in Gandhi's ashram in India in order to learn from him how to solve political conflicts without employing force. And in 1939, when he saw so clearly that the war was coming, he could easily have stayed in America; his friends there did their utmost to keep him. But if he had done so, it would have been a denial of everything he had said about concrete discipleship. So he went back to Germany. However, he was still thinking about passive resistance. In 1939, when I paced up and down the platform with him at Paddington Station in London, the main subject of our conversation was, if the Hitler government started a war and he were called up, whether he should not become a conscientious objector. What was it that made him decide to take the

grave step of participating very actively in preparing the events which culminated in the coup d'etat of July 20, 1944? Here again the answer is that for him it was all or nothing. He did not like half-measures. He could not confine himself to rejecting the Nazi regime in theory, nor withdraw into a sphere of pure thought. Such an attitude would be a form of schizophrenia, a failure to respond to the call for *action* (not for talking). He had suffered from the fact that the church struggle was primarily a struggle for self-preservation. In such a situation, in which the lives of millions of people were threatened, the essential point was not to save the church. It was to save mankind in distress. The same conviction which had made him a man of peace now led him to take active resistance.

For him resistance meant rescue-action. The task was not merely to destroy the Nazi system, but also to establish a just international order. It was in this spirit that Bonhoeffer and I met in Geneva in September 1941 and worked out together a memorandum on the peace-aims which could be jointly advocated by a Christian from Germany and a Christian from Holland. On that occasion he was very frank. He said it would depend very much on whether a new German government could count on the immediate political support of the Allies. But he did not mean that as a political bargain. He was not like those generals who keep on hesitating for the right opportunity, for a better strategic or diplomatic situation. He was concerned with a deeper necessity. That was why he said in 1940, in a conversation which came to the ears of the Bishop of Chichester: "If we claim to be Christians, we must not be influenced by tactical considerations." And in 1942, when in Sweden, he added: "Our action must be of such a kind that the world will understand it as an act of atonement." He expressed the same thought to us in a small group of friends in Geneva: "It is only through defeat that we can atone for the horrible crimes which we have committed against Europe and against the world." Was that fanatical idealism? No, it was simply putting into practice the biblical truth which applies to all nations: "What is a man profited, if he shall gain the whole world, and lose his own soul?" (Matt. 16:26, KJV)

Bonhoeffer loved his fatherland. But for that very reason he found it intolerable that it should plunge into ever deeper guilt. It was not enough to weep and lament. In such a situation a Christian man must try to seize the mad horse, and stop it, even if it appeared almost impossible. No, he was no fanatic. Trained politicians had already come to the same conclusion. But was it not all in vain, after all, because the German resistance movement was not taken seriously by the Allies? I know from my own experience in London in 1942, when I transmitted a memorandum drawn up by the German resistance movement to the British government, that both

in 1942 and in July 1944 the attitude of the Allied governments was very shortsighted. But history continued, and today there are many people in the world who are deeply grateful that just when events were most terrible men still existed in Germany who showed that there was still another Germany. Through the complete altruism of his action and through his death Bonhoeffer foreshadowed the Stuttgart Declaration of Guilt and confirmed it. By doing so he made an important contribution to reconciliation in the years after the war.

Last but not least, we must speak of another Bonhoeffer—the man who in his prison cell worked out entirely new, revolutionary ideas about Christianity and the world, telling us that the new "adult" world has become an "irreligious" world which is no longer willing or able to listen to the gospel, and that the church must stop defending itself and its particular "religiosity" and simply *be present* in the world for others, as Jesus Christ was. Has this Bonhoeffer still anything in common with the man who struggled against the temporal authorities and rejected all compromise between the church and the world? At the very end did he abandon the decided views which were characteristics of his life? Personally I am convinced that no break occurred in his faith and in his thinking; he was merely working out ideas which he had always had, and carrying them farther. Already in 1932 he had said: "The

whole world belongs to Christ, not merely one sacred, religious sphere within it." He had always protested against the fact that the church defends its own existence instead of being prepared to live and die for the world. He always preached a "cosmic" gospel, in the true sense. In his *Ethics*, written during his last years, he quotes the first chapter of the letter to the Colossians more than any other biblical passage. In 1941 when we were working on the memorandum for England, he formulated the basis of a new world-order in the following words: "Because the world exists only 'in Christ' and 'for Christ' (Colossians), any view of man 'for himself alone' is a mere abstraction. In accordance with the will of God, everything is related to Christ, whether this is realized or not." And in the letter written in August 1944 he says, briefly and clearly: "Everything depends on the words 'in Christ.'" Therefore he had not stopped thinking in a radically Christocentric way. He only perceived still more clearly that Christ wants to break out of the systems, traditions, and institutions in which men have tried to enclose him. The point is not that a sort of "extra-territorial" church exists, side by side with the world. The point is that men and women, whether they have religious needs or not, "let themselves be drawn into the way of Jesus Christ, into the Messianic Event, . . . into the Messianic suffering of God in Jesus Christ."

The challenge thrown down by

Bonhoeffer's last letters, which can so easily be misunderstood, therefore does not mean that we cover up the stumbling block of the God who became man in Jesus, and try to find a gospel that is easier for modern, "adult" people to believe. The challenge means that we must understand the incarnation really radically. Christ did not bear the sins of Christians; he bore the sins of the world. The church must therefore live and suffer in the world, with the world, for the world.

We shall never have done with Bonhoeffer. His questions and his insights will go on demanding our attention. All over the world people who are trying to find meaning and joy in life despite the disorder of the world are listening attentively to what he says, because he was granted the great opportunity of confirming his message through his life and his death.

W. A. Visser 't Hooft
Geneva, Switzerland

Although Everyman must walk through the streets of his own milieu and is destined, inescapably, to be part of the culture into which he was born, few men have been so much a part of their times as was Dietrich Bonhoeffer. And few—including the great statesmen of the past—have contributed so persuasively and so penetratingly to the thought patterns and life styles of other persons.

The second assertion follows from the first. It is precisely because the German pastor was so much at home in the troubled world of the 1930s and early 1940s that other men, struggling against the undertow of history, have grasped his teachings as though they were the only buoyant force in sight. This itself is ironic, for Bonhoeffer was at home not only in the tempest of life but the finality of death, which he anticipated as the "highest of feasts on the way to freedom."

Not that Dietrich (whose Christian name springs to the lips of any person who reads his *Letters* and the reminiscences of his friends) despised the pleasures of living. He loved simple things: the echoes of hymns which occasionally invaded the heavy masonry of his prison cell, a bouquet of dahlias, a good book, the chance to encourage a fearful fellow-prisoner. He was close to his family and looked forward tenderly to a marriage that never took place. He recalled the joys of travel: conversations among the dunes along the

Baltic, holidays in the Harz Mountains, a pilgrimage to Rome, the journey by auto from New York City to Chicago and thence to Mexico City. And Dietrich thoroughly enjoyed people. The poignance of Harlem Negroes drew his spirit more than the magnificence of the metropolis. At a time when his lectures at the University of Berlin were bringing smiles to the lips of students and controversy to the church, he gave himself energetically to a confirmation class of fifty boys in one of Berlin's least desirable neighborhoods. Even his prison warders received his gentle ministries.

His whole life was of a piece. W. A. Visser 't Hooft has called him the "least schizophrenic of men." Yet Bonhoeffer's complete identification with his time was most clearly demonstrated when he forsook the congenial safety of an American campus to return to the Fatherland. In the midst of a people swept off their feet emotionally, the courageous pastor took his determined stand against a crazed but seemingly omnipotent dictator.

How foolhardy his benefactors must have considered the young man whom they had brought to America at personal sacrifice! In the steamy heat of a summer night in 1939, Dietrich had walked up and down Times Square, agonizing over the news from Europe. Alone, he sought to reject the cup of suffering he knew would be his. Next day, June 20, he wrote to Reinhold Niebuhr, "I have come to the conclusion that I have made

a mistake in coming to America. I must live through this difficult period of our national history with the Christian people of Germany. I will have no right to participate in the reconstruction of Christian life in Germany after the war if I do not share the trials of this same time with my people."

Henry Smith Leiper, then secretary of the Federal Council of Churches, had collected several thousand dollars to bring Dietrich to the States and considered him "the right man at the right time" for certain tasks in America. Later, Leiper compared Bonhoeffer with Jesus "who had, long centuries ago, taken the road to Golgotha as he 'set his face steadfastly toward Jerusalem.'"

Once home, the distressed theologian wrestled with his convictions, plotted against *der Führer*, joined the Counterespionage as a cover for continued contact with Christians in Switzerland, Sweden, and England, was arrested, imprisoned, and finally executed. After two years behind bars, Bonhoeffer died less than a month before Hitler committed suicide.

If the quiet example of Bonhoeffer's life stirred the hearts of those whose vocations coincided with his, the forceful logic of his writings provided a rationale. In retrospect it can be said that his *Cost of Discipleship* and *Life Together* were for the resistance movement among German Christians what *Mein Kampf* was to the misled *Reich*. So great a threat was this man's teachings to history's most ruthless dictator that by August 5, 1936,

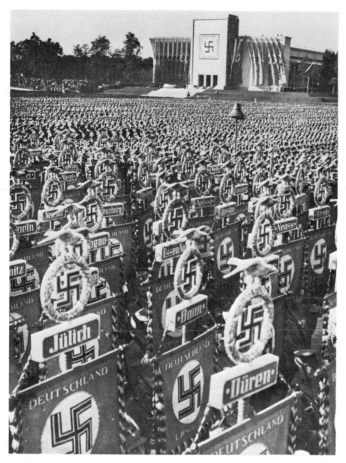

Banners of storm troops, Nuremberg, September 1936

Military parade, Berlin, April 1939

The World's Fair opened in New York in May 1939, dedicated to Peace and Unity among nations and to the progress of democracy.

Most of the German nation was committed by an oath of loyalty to Hitler and was embarked on a path that had already begun to shatter the peace of Europe.

Court of Peace, World's Fair, 1939

Bonhoeffer was denied the right to lecture at the University. Later he was restrained from speaking in public anywhere, and the publication of his books was forbidden.

Both critics and disciples have claimed that Bonhoeffer was ahead of his time in perceiving with a kind of clairvoyance the relentless march of secularism and pioneering a politically oriented expression of the Christian ethic. He taught that the world should dictate the church's agenda long before that slogan was conceived. He struggled to define a "religionless Christianity" two decades before his fragmentary writings were seized and distorted by the theologians who proclaimed "the death of God" so profitably.

Without doubt, Bonhoeffer was among the first to see the nature of "a world come of age," of a "post-Christian" church and society, as well as the high "cost of discipleship." He caused men to puzzle when he stated the paradox "before (as it were, in the face of, or in the presence of) and with God we live without God."

But it is an error to assert that Dietrich Bonhoeffer was ahead of his time. More than the vast audiences who roared their approval of their charismatic though demented *Führer*, Bonhoeffer accepted the drama of history for what it was. And he played his own part without script or prompting.

Similarly it is wrong to caricature him as "the apostle of Christian atheism." To do so erects a whole system of theology (which his untimely death prohibited him

from doing) on a fragmentary, albeit significant, expression of his thought. The true Bonhoeffer is to be observed in his convictions about the incarnation. "There are not two realities but only one reality," he declared in his *Ethics*. "This is the reality of God in the reality of the world, revealed in Christ. Participating in Christ, we stand at one and the same time in the reality of God and in the reality of the world. The reality of Christ includes within itself the reality of the world. . . . It is a denial of the revelation of God in Jesus Christ to wish to be 'Christian' without seeing and recognizing the world in Christ."

Dietrich's own life was lived according to this understanding. His deeply biblical faith caused him to leave the pulpit behind and to become involved in the ultimate of political action; his convictions led him to help plot an attempt on Hitler's life and to communicate regularly with the enemies of the Third *Reich*. Thousands have seen these acts, and the martyrdom to which they led, as an inspiring contemporary example of incarnation, of faith in action.

Dietrich was a deeply religious man, in the style of an enlightened pietism. His letters are laced with biblical texts which he found meaningful, comforting, or provocative. So sensitive was he to the spiritual hunger of his fellow prisoners that the chaplain at Tegel asked him to compose prayers for the inmates. Hymns which he had memorized long before echoed through his conscious and subconscious being.

Bonhoeffer had just led a brief devotional service at the prison in Schönberg when the Black Guards of the SS led him away to be court-martialed and hanged. The doctor who witnessed the execution recorded that Bonhoeffer knelt in his cell, "praying fervently," before removing his prison garb. There was another short prayer at the foot of the scaffold. "Then," Dr. H. Fischer-Hüllstrung recalled, Bonhoeffer "climbed the steps to the gallows, brave and composed. . . . In the almost fifty years that I have worked as a doctor, I have hardly ever seen a man die so entirely submissive to the will of God."

Dietrich himself had described the religious man as "this-worldly" rather than in the sentimental or escapist terms so common in Germany and America at that time. On July 21, 1944 (the day after the coup d'état failed), Bonhoeffer wrote to his friend Eberhard Bethge, "I simply take pleasure in the day's *Losungen* [Bible texts] . . . and I am always glad to go back to Paul Gerhardt's beautiful hymns. During the last year or so I have come to know and understand more and more the profound this-worldliness of Christianity. The Christian is not a *homo religiosus*, but simply a man, as Jesus was a man—in contrast, shall we say, to John the Baptist. I don't mean the shallow and banal this-worldliness of the enlightened, the busy, the comfortable, or the lascivious, but the profound this-worldliness characterized by discipline and the constant knowledge of death and resurrection. I think Luther lived a this-worldly life in this sense."

Places, as well as people and events, were important to the preacher who deliberately chose to return to Germany. "The 'among us,' the 'now' and 'here' is therefore the region of our decisions and encounters," he wrote. "In our historical identity, therefore, we stand already in the midst of Christ's taking form, in a section of human history which he, himself, has chosen."

The incarnation, for Bonhoeffer, meant Christ's involvement in history—contemporary as well as past. It meant God's concern about the terrible and concrete events of that day and that country. And it meant God's participation—through those who were faithful to him—in challenging and eventually in changing the unholy forces currently in power.

It is not strange that a generation later, with the world still reeling from the events of the past and possessing even more awesome weapons of destruction, the price this man paid for discipleship and the eloquence of his witness should command the interest and respect of laymen and scholars alike. A whole shelf of resources has been developed so that we may see Dietrich Bonhoeffer within the historic context of the world's reaction to Hitler. Books, papers, lectures, sermons, and the like have been written to provide insight into the times and people which shaped Bonhoeffer's life. But no similar effort has been made to deal with the places which he himself described so effectively in his writings. This volume attempts to fill that void.

We begin, of course, by recognizing that for the most part Bonhoeffer worked behind the scenes.

The seminary he headed was clandestine, its methods and various locations shrouded in secrecy. He was able, by joining the counter-intelligence, to travel with immunity as he made contact with Christian leaders in other nations. Some of his writings were confiscated, others were hidden until after the war. Because he was a public figure in a private setting, the photographs taken during those critical years show little or nothing of places. Only persons. The collection gathered in this book were taken twenty-three years after Bonhoeffer's death. They show what is left: scars of bitterness and brutality, memorials to men of conviction, and an eloquent testimony that life goes on, enriched by men like Dietrich Bonhoeffer, whose feet paced the same streets years before.

J. Martin Bailey

Germany, 1929

DENMARK

BALTIC SEA

NORTH SEA

Danzig

E. PRUSSIA

Zingst

Stölp

Griefswald

Schlawe

Köslin

Hamburg

POMERANIA

Finkenwalde

Schwerin

Stettin

NETHERLANDS

Berlin

POLAND

BELGIUM

Wuppertal

Buchenwald
Concentration Camp

Flossenbürg

CZECHOSLOVAKIA

Nürenberg

Schwäbisch Hall

Regensburg

Schönberg

FRANCE

Passau

Stuttgart

Tübingen

Munich

AUSTRIA

HUNGARY

SWITZERLAND

Chronology of Events and Places

BIRTH	February 4, 1906	Dietrich and Sabine Bonhoeffer born in Breslau to Dr. and Mrs. Karl Bonhoeffer
AGE 6	1912	Family moves to Berlin where father teaches neurology and psychiatry and heads University Hospital
7	1913	Dietrich enters *Gymnasium*
15	March 15, 1921	Dietrich and Sabine confirmed at Grunewald Church, Berlin
17	1923	Dietrich begins theological studies at Tübingen; visits ancestral home in Schwäbish Hall
21	December 17, 1927	Dietrich receives licentiate in theology
22	February 15, 1928	Begins year as curate in Barcelona, Spain
24	July 31, 1930	Presents inaugural lecture at Berlin (Humboldt) University
	September 5, 1930	Leaves for New York to study at Union Theological Seminary
25	August 1, 1931	Becomes lecturer in theology at Berlin University
	October 1, 1931	Becomes chaplain at Technical College, Berlin
	November 15, 1931	Ordained at Matthäis Church
26	November 1931 to March 1932	Teaches confirmation class at Zion Church, Berlin-Wedding
	August 1932	Participates in ecumenical conferences
	January 30, 1933	Adolph Hitler becomes *Reich* Chancellor
	February 1, 1933	Dietrich's radio talk, "Changes in the Concept of the Leader Principle," is cut off the air before completion

	February 27, 1933	Reichstag fire
27	April 1933	Storm troops begin systematic attacks on Jews. Non-Aryans (including Dietrich's brother-in-law) eliminated from public life and professions. Dietrich publishes essay, "The Church and the Jewish Problem."
	September 7, 1933	Dietrich collaborates with Martin Niemöller on Pastors' Emergency League
	October 17, 1933	Begins two-year pastorate at the Reformed Church of St. Paul and the German Evangelical Church in Sydenham, London; develops friendship with Bishop G. K. A. Bell of Chichester. Begins writing *The Cost of Discipleship.*
28	November 5, 1934	London congregation breaks with *Reich* Church
	November 25, 1934	Dietrich visits Brethren Council prior to synod of the Confessing Church
29	April 26, 1935	Dietrich founds clandestine Preachers' Seminary for Confessing Church at Zingsthof on Baltic Sea
	June 24, 1935	Seminary moves to Finkenwalde, near Stettin, in Pomerania; *Bruderhaus* built in Finkenwalde
	September 1935	Nuremberg Laws cancel citizenship for all German Jews, forbid marriage between Jews and Aryans
30	February 1936	Dietrich lectures in Berlin on discipleship
	March 7, 1936	Hitler occupies demilitarized zone of Rhineland
	August 1–5, 1936	Olympics at Berlin. Dietrich preaches at Olympic Village.
	August 5, 1936	Dietrich denied right to lecture at University
	November 13, 1936	Finkenwalde student arrested and

		taken to concentration camp on eve of ordination
31	Mid-October, 1937	Finkenwalde Seminary closed by Gestapo
	November 1937	Twenty-seven former Finkenwalde students imprisoned
		Dietrich publishes *The Cost of Discipleship*
	December 5, 1937	Team curacies are established to continue clandestine training of clergy for Confessing Church
32	February 1938	Dietrich makes first contacts with Sack, Oster, Canaris, and Beck in connection with plot against Hitler
	March 13, 1938	Germany annexes Austria
	September 1938	Dietrich writes *Life Together;* sees twin sister Sabine and her husband, Gerhard Leibholz, a Jew, off for safety in London
	September 30, 1938	Munich agreement for peace in Europe signed by Hitler and Neville Chamberlain
	November 9, 1938	*Krystallnacht.* Simultaneous destruction of 600 German synagogues, looting of 7,500 shops, and arrest of 35,000 Jews
	January 1, 1939	All Jewish businesses liquidated by Göring
33	March 10, 1939	Dietrich visits with Bell, Reinhold Niebuhr, W. A. Visser 't Hooft, and Leibholz in London
	March 14, 1939	Hitler marches into Czechoslovakia
	June 2, 1939	Dietrich leaves for New York, stopping in London for final visit with Sabine
	July 27, 1939	As tensions mount in Europe, Dietrich decides to return to his people
	September 1, 1939	Germany invades Poland; France and

		Great Britain declare war two days later
34	March 17, 1940	Gestapo closes team curacies in Sigurdshoff
	April 9, 1940	Germany invades Denmark and Norway
	May 10, 1940	Germany invades Holland, Belgium, and France
	August 1940	Dietrich discusses service in Counterespionage with Oster and his brother-in-law Dr. Hans von Dohnanyi
	September 9, 1940	Dietrich is ordered to report to Gestapo and forbidden to speak in public. He begins work on *Ethics*.
	November 17, 1940	Dietrich is guest of Benedictine Abbey at Ettal while awaiting orders from Counterespionage; he continues work on *Ethics*
35	June 22, 1941	Germany invades Soviet Union
	December 11, 1941	Germany declares war on U.S.A.
	1942	Hitler is committed to "Final Solution to the Jewish Problem." Dietrich undertakes two journeys to Switzerland; makes contact with Visser 't Hooft.
36	1942	Dietrich journeys to Norway, Sweden, Switzerland for Counterespionage
	May 30 to June 2, 1942	Meets Bishop Bell in Stockholm and Sigtuna
	January 1943	German army surrenders at Stalingrad
	January 17, 1943	Dietrich becomes engaged to Maria von Wedemeyer
37	April 5, 1943	House at Marienburger Allee 43 is searched; Dietrich is arrested and taken to Tegel; Hans von Dohnanyi and Josef Müller and their wives also are arrested
	May 13, 1943	German-Italian forces surrender in North Africa

38	June 6, 1944	Allies land at Normandy
	July 20, 1944	Attempt on Hitler's life fails
	October 8, 1944	Dietrich transferred to cellar of Gestapo prison in Prinz Albrecht Strasse
	January 15, 1945	Red armies invade East Prussia
39	February 7, 1945	Dietrich transferred to Buchenwald Concentration Camp
	March 7, 1945	Allied armies cross the Rhine
	April 3, 1945	Moved from Buchenwald to Regensburg
	April 6, 1945	Moved to Schönberg
	April 8, 1945	Transported to Flossenbürg; court-martialed the same night
	April 9, 1945	On Himmler's orders, Oster, Sack, Canaris, Strünck, Gehre, and Dietrich Bonhoeffer hanged at Flossenbürg. Hans von Dohnanyi killed in Sachsenhausen.
	April 23, 1945	Klaus Bonhoeffer murdered by Gestapo in Berlin with Rüdiger Schleicher, the husband of Ursula Bonhoeffer. Red army reaches Berlin.
	April 30, 1945	Hitler commits suicide
	May 7, 1945	Germany surrenders

1

The Secret of Freedom

SELF-DISCIPLINE

If you set out to seek freedom, you must learn before all things
Mastery over sense and soul, lest your wayward desirings,
Lest your undisciplined members lead you now this way, now that way.
Chaste be your mind and your body, and subject to you and obedient,
Serving solely to seek their appointed goal and objective.
None learns the secret of freedom save only by way of control.

he self-discipline which Dietrich Bonhoeffer developed during his childhood and student years provided the matrix for his life of action and suffering which followed. Even the seeds of his theological perceptions were present in the style, the ideals, the friends, and the intellectual context of his parents' home in Berlin.

Persons, rather than things, were important in their upper-middle-class household. Although Karl and Paula Bonhoeffer were strict with their children, the youngsters were encouraged to pursue their own interests. Dietrich's twin sister, Sabine, has described the little workshop which her brothers used and another room which they made into a veritable zoo for snakes, lizards, and beetles, as well as a museum of butterflies and birds' eggs.

Karl taught his children by example. He was a generous, disciplined, quiet man who expected a great deal from his four sons and four daughters. The children responded to the sense of humor with which he teased them out of their inhibitions. His patience was rewarded, for he enjoyed watching his youngsters grow and develop their own concerns within a home which was intellectually and esthetically rich. As Dietrich observed his doctor father's devotion to his patients and his tireless search for the most effective treatment, the youth developed his own sense of compassion. Once he "preached" a little sermon to his father when he discovered that pa-

tients were sent bills: "You shouldn't accept money from sick people."

Religion was seldom mentioned in the home, although the family conformed to the traditions of the church and although the noted church historian Adolf von Harnack was a neighborhood friend. Yet Christian ideals and the joys of fellowship pervaded the household. Although there was no surprise in Dietrich's theological inclinations, there was nothing sentimental or pietistic in the response of his family either. There was, at

first, a lack of appreciation for the choice he had made; but never was a discouraging word spoken. Later he was able to articulate his inbred concern for the secular. He determined to make his witness in actions rather than words (though memorable phrases flowed from his pen). He longed to serve effectively.

The family's better-than-average means made it possible for Dietrich to travel. He studied theology at Tübingen when he was only seventeen, served as a curate in Spain five years later, and spent a year

Woodcut—Luther at Worms

Luther in his trial at Worms had already framed a reply which Dietrich was to relive and revivify in his own life. Luther had said, "I do not accept the authority of popes and councils, for they have contradicted one another—my conscience is captive to the Word of God. I cannot and I will not recant anything, for to go against conscience is neither right nor safe. God help me. Amen."

at Union Theological Seminary in New York before settling in as a pastor and professor. His travels to ecumenical student assemblies and a period of preaching in London made him an internationalist. Once, at a youth conference in Denmark, he spoke of the emerging ecumenical church as "the indestructible community," and of "the impossibility of bearing arms against him who has become our brother in Christ, and in whom Christ himself would be hit."

Bonhoeffer's early life was a disciplined blending of free inquiry, cultural enrichment, intensive study, energetic play, and relaxed good humor. His love for books and his powers of intellectual concentration enabled him to remain lucid and creative throughout a long and worrisome imprisonment. He enjoyed music and art and he carried their images with him wherever he walked "on the way to freedom." He learned this discipline at home and in school. It became part of his nature. It was his life style. He kept it to the end.

The Bonhoeffer family home at Wangenheim Strasse 14 in Berlin provided a place where the young professor could entertain his students in mind and body. To one, who was embarrassed by being asked to stay for a meal, Dietrich replied, "That is not just my bread, it is *our* bread, and when it is jointly consumed there will still be twelve baskets left over."

In 1918 Bonhoeffer's parents moved to a pleasant home at Wangenheim Strasse 14 in Grunewald, Berlin.

It happens to be the case that certain things remain unsaid in my family, while they are expressed in yours. There is no point discussing what is the "right" way. It involves different people who act as they inwardly must. I can imagine that at first it will be hard for you that many things, especially in religious matters, remain unexpressed at home. But I would be very glad if you could succeed in adjusting to the ways of my parents as I have tried through your grandmother to adjust to the ways of your family. I have become increasingly grateful for this.

You are the first of a new generation in our family, and therefore the oldest representative of your generation. You will have the priceless advantage of spending a good part of your life with the third and fourth generation that went before you. Your great-grandfather will be able to tell you, from his own personal memories, of people who were born in the eighteenth century; and one day, long after the year 2000, you will be the living bridge over which your descendants will get an oral tradition of more than 250 years—all this sub conditione Jacobea, *"if the Lord wills." So your birth provides us with a suitable occasion to reflect on the changes that time brings, and to try to scan the outlines of the future.*

Michaelskirche in Schwäbisch Hall, where the ancestors of Karl Bonhoeffer are buried

Conscience comes from a depth which lies beyond a man's own will and his own reason and it makes itself heard as the call of human existence to unity with itself. Conscience comes as an indictment of the loss of this unity and as a warning against the loss of one's self. . . . When the national socialist says, "My conscience is Adolf Hitler," that, too, is an attempt to find a foundation for the unity of his own ego somewhere beyond himself. The consequence of this is the surrender of one's autonomy for the sake of an unconditional heteronomy, and this in turn is possible only if the other man, the man to whom I look for the unity of my life, fulfills the function of a redeemer for me. This, then, provides an extremely direct and significant parallel to the Christian truth, and at the same time an extremely direct and significant contrast with it.

"Igel" fraternity house, where Dietrich lived as a student at Tübingen. He resigned from the fraternity when it adopted Hitler's Aryan policies.

Berlin University, now called Humboldt
University, in the Eastern Zone

Every possible piece of furniture in Wolf-Dieter Zimmermann's student apartment in Berlin was used to seat the students who gathered weekly for an open discussion with their Humboldt University professor, Dietrich Bonhoeffer. Zimmermann remembers only one of the subjects discussed, "What is a sacrament and what does it effect?", for the major thrust of the discussion was to teach the students to think logically and to theologize. Afterward, in a beer cellar, as guests of their professor, the students discussed such topical questions as the church struggle in Germany.

Student apartment near Humboldt University, used by Wolf-Dieter Zimmermann and his friends

The day of the Lord's Supper is an occasion of joy for the Christian community. Reconciled in their hearts with God and the brethren, the congregation receives the gift of the body and blood of Jesus Christ, and, receiving that, it receives forgiveness, new life, and salvation. It is given new fellowship with God and men. The fellowship of the Lord's Supper is the superlative fulfillment of Christian fellowship. As the members of the congregation are united in body and blood at the table of the Lord so will they be together in eternity. Here the community has reached its goal. Here joy in Christ and his community is complete. The life of Christians together under the Word has reached its perfection in the sacrament.

In a conversation with his professor, Wolf-Dieter Zimmermann once inquired about a certain book. "You can have it," Bonhoeffer offered. When the young student protested that he dare not carry off a professor's book, Bonhoeffer asked, "What on earth is your idea of property?"

Bonhoeffer was moved deeply by his contacts with American Negroes. He carried records of their spirituals back to Germany and played them for his students. He described traveling through the States with a colored friend: how hotels and restaurants refused admittance to them. He saw, even in the early '30s, that the piety, worship, and theology of American Negroes would provide a new reformation.

Negro churches in Harlem, New York

What a blessing it is, in such distressing times, to belong to a large, closely knit family, where each trusts the other and stands by him. When pastors were arrested, I sometimes used to think that it must be easiest for those of them who were unmarried. But I did not know then what the warmth that radiates from the love of a wife and family can mean in the cold air of imprisonment, and how in just such times of separation the feeling of belonging together through thick and thin actually grows stronger . . .

Sabine Liebholz, Dietrich's twin, who has lived in Karlsruhe since 1956. Her husband is a professor of law.

It is becoming clearer every day that the most urgent problem besetting our church is this: How can we live the Christian life in the modern world?

Happy are they who have reached the end of the road we seek to tread, who are astonished to discover the by no means self-evident truth that grace is costly just because it is the grace of God in Jesus Christ. Happy are the simple followers of Jesus Christ who have been overcome by his grace, and are able to sing the praises of the all-sufficient grace of Christ with humbleness of heart. Happy are they who, knowing that grace, can live in the world without being of it, who, by following Jesus Christ, are so assured of their heavenly citizenship that they are truly free to live their lives in this world. Happy are they who know that discipleship simply means the life which springs from grace, and that grace simply means discipleship. Happy are they who have become Christians in this sense of the word. For them the word of grace has proved a fount of mercy.

Matthäis Church, Berlin, where Bonhoeffer
was ordained in 1931

2

The Tempest of Living

ACTION

Do and dare what is right, not swayed by the whim of the moment.
Bravely take hold of the real, not dallying now with what might be.
Not in the flight of ideas but only in action is freedom.
Make up your mind and come out into the tempest of living.
God's command is enough and your faith in him to sustain you.
Then at last freedom will welcome your spirit amid great rejoicing.

Although the roots of Dietrich Bonhoeffer's discipleship were anchored deeply in the soil of German culture and scholarship, it was the stormy climate of his times that encouraged the rapid development of his convictions and provided the arena for his actions. The influence of his parents and teachers was great, but it was Adolf Hitler who stimulated the theologian to do and to dare what he considered right.

Shortly after Dietrich completed his studies and was ordained in the German Evangelical Church, the world witnessed the rise of the "hysterical orator with the pasty face, the wild eyes, the unruly forelock, and the absurd smudge of a moustache." It was easy for most persons to underestimate this son of a semiliterate Austrian shoemaker and the freebooters, political murderers, and middle-class riffraff he organized into the National Socialist German Workers' Party. Between 1929 and 1933 the world was preoccupied with a pervasive economic crisis. Unlike most of his countrymen, Bonhoeffer saw through the storms of rage and the promises of a millenial Third *Reich* expressed in the crude and gutteral voice of Hitler.

Two days after *der Führer* became *Reich* Chancellor on January 30, 1933, Dietrich's radio lecture on "Changes in the Concept of the Leader Principle" was cut off the air. Three months later, as the man who described himself in *Mein Kampf* as "having been transformed from a weak world-citizen into a fanatic anti-Semite" began eliminating non-Aryans from public and professional life, the twenty-seven-year-old minister published an essay on "The Church and the Jewish problem." In August of that year he helped draft the "Bethel Confession," and in September he joined Martin Niemöller in planning for the Pastors' Emergency League.

His revulsion for Hitler and the way in which the *Reich* Church had been seduced and intimidated by *der Führer* led Bonhoeffer to accept a two-year pastorate in London. During that time the German-speaking congregation he served broke ties with the *Reich* Church and Bonhoeffer developed an intimate friendship with the Anglican Bishop George K. A. Bell of Chichester. He helped the ecumenically minded Bell, and other Englishmen, to understand the dimensions of the church struggle in Germany as well as the gathering tempest on the continent.

In these anxious times, the earnest pastor began writing *The Cost of Discipleship* and was drawn to the magnetic personality and pacific spirit of Gandhi. Bishop Bell arranged for him to visit India and to interview the Mahatma but, just before the journey, Dietrich received an urgent call to return home and to open an underground seminary.

The Preachers' Seminary he founded soon moved from Zingsthof to Finkenwalde in Pomerania. And, two and one-half years after he opened the clandestine school, twenty-seven of the students were in prison, Dietrich had been forbidden to lecture at the University, and the Finkenwalde *Bruderhaus* had been closed by the secret police. But by the end of 1937 Dietrich had published his controversial book on discipleship and had helped to establish "team curacies" to continue training leaders for the Confessing Church.

The mobilization of Germany and the increasing pressures on Jewish citizens led the theologian to the conviction that Hitler would have to be eliminated. Shortly before Austria was annexed by the *Reich*, Dietrich made contact with four men who began an elaborate plot against *der Führer*.

Throughout Europe war fever spread rapidly. In September Dietrich wrote his treatise on devotion, *Life Together*, and bade farewell to his twin sister Sabine and her Jewish husband, who emigrated to England. Within a matter of weeks 600 synagogues were destroyed, 7,500 Jewish shops were looted, 35,000 Jews were arrested and, on January 1, 1939, all Jewish businesses were liquidated by Göring.

As tensions mounted, Dietrich felt torn by his desire to get away from the hatred and ugliness of his native country and his passion to help restore reason and moral values. He joined the many German intellectuals who sought haven in the United States, only to feel compelled to return to his people. "I do not understand why I am here," he wrote in his diary. "The short prayer in which we thought of our German brothers almost overwhelmed me. If things become more uncertain, I shall certainly go back to Germany. . . . If war comes, I shall not stay in America." On one of the last ships to sail before the war broke out he reflected, "Since I came on board ship, my mental turmoil about the future has gone."

An ironic double life followed. After the team curacies were rooted out by the Gestapo, the forthright pastor was deprived the right to speak in public. But, oddly, he was employed—through a conspiracy involving his brother-in-law Hans von Dohnanyi and General Oster of the foreign office—by the *Abwehr* or Counterespionage. Traveling with an official passport and at government expense, Dietrich several times visited Switzerland as well as Norway and Sweden. On these secret visits he main-

tained contact with church leaders, including those who already were preparing for the formation of the World Council of Churches at the end of the war.

Learning through the underground of the presence in Sweden of his friend Bishop Bell, Dietrich met the British churchman behind closed doors and appealed for official Allied assurances that the war would be ended immediately if the attempt on Hitler's life were successful. The Bishop of Chichester relayed the message to the British Foreign Minister, Anthony Eden, but by that time the Allies were committed to a policy of unconditional surrender.

Before the assassination could be attempted Dietrich was arrested, and many of his papers were confiscated.

Relentlessly, the tempest of life

had swept Dietrich Bonhoeffer into the vortex of history. Yet the young German Christian—who wrestled all during these dangerous days with a volume on *Ethics* which he never completed—had stepped deliberately into the arena. "Not in the flight of ideas but only in action is freedom," he was convinced, just as he believed that Germany should be appropriately punished. "Christians," he told Bishop Bell at Sigtuna, in Sweden, "do not wish to escape repentance, or chaos, if it is God's will to bring it on us. We must take this judgment as Christians."

For Dietrich, God's command was enough. For him, faith in God was sustaining, even in the perilous events in which he was involved.

Political campaign of Hitler at Nuremberg in 1929. He campaigned to arouse anti-Communist and anti-Semitic fears. By the end of 1932, the Nazi Party had won a majority of seats in the Reichstag and Hitler had become Chancellor of the Reich.

More than 100,000 Socialists and trade unionists demonstrated against Hitler in October 1930. When Hitler came to power the trade unions were dissolved and their leaders as well as leaders of opposition parties were arrested.

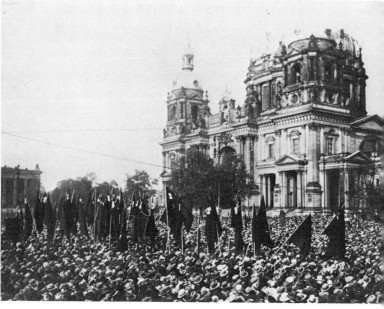

The burning of the Reichstag in February 1933 was the excuse for the emergency decrees which remained in effect during Hitler's lifetime. These suppressed all individual freedom.

By 1935 the SS, Hitler's elite troops acting for the army, had remilitarized the Rhineland and broken the Versailles Treaty.

Book burning took place throughout Germany for ten weeks in 1933. Nazi university youth conducted this attack on intellectual freedom.

By 1933 official harassment of the Jews had swept throughout Germany.

Hitler organized all German youth in a nationalist, government-directed program. All other youth organizations were made illegal.

Torchlight parade of Hitler Youth in Berlin, January 1935

On May Day 1936, Hitler had completely marshaled the German people into a militaristic state glorifying his Third Reich.

In 1936 Hitler still beguiled the world and found international acceptance of his regime as host to the Olympic Games.

During the Olympics, signs such as this one were removed wherever foreign visitors were expected. Persecution of the Confessing Church ceased for two weeks and Dietrich and Niemöller were allowed to preach at the Olympic Village.

In January 1936, before the International Olympic Games, Hitler's "sports clubs" were conducting preparatory training for war.

In 1938 renewed attacks on the Jews warned all citizens to avoid trading with them.

Hitler's personal magnetism and organizing brilliance had completely reduced the Reich to a monolithic, depersonalized, military government. Nuremberg Rally, September 1938

The West was lulled by Chamberlain's agreement with Hitler at the "Peace of Munich" on September 30, 1938.

44

On March 14, 1939 Hitler's army occupied Prague.

On September 1, 1939 Hitler invaded Poland and war was declared by France and Great Britain. On September 2, 1939 Hitler bombed Warsaw and claimed he was attacking "military objectives."

During the tense year of 1932, Dietrich Bonhoeffer found time to teach a group of fifty boys in the confirmation class of Zion Church in a slum section of Berlin known as Wedding. Richard Rother, one of the boys, recalls how their pastor took a room in the neighborhood in order to be near the group.

The confirmands were greatly impressed by Bonhoeffer's confidence in them, expressed by his explicit instructions to his landlady to allow the boys into his room in his absence. At the peak of the depression, Bonhoeffer took ten boys from what Rother has called the "stony desert of the city" for a two-week holiday in the Harz Mountains.

House at Oderberger Strasse 61, in Berlin-Wedding, where Bonhoeffer lived while teaching confirmation class at Zion Church

Honesty demands that we recognize that we must live in the world as if there were no God. And this is just what we do recognize—before God! God himself drives us to this realization.—God makes us know that we must live as men who can get along without him. The God who is with us is the God who forsakes us (Mark 15:34)! We stand continually in the presence of the God who makes us live in the world without the God-hypothesis.

Zion Church in Berlin-Wedding, where Bonhoeffer taught confirmation class

Privation is the lot of the disciples in every sphere of their lives. They are the "poor" tout court (Luke 6:20). They have no security, no possessions to call their own, not even a foot of earth to call their home, no earthly society to claim their absolute allegiance. Nay more, they have no spiritual power, experience, or knowledge to afford them consolation or security. For his sake they have lost all. In following him they lost even their own selves, and everything that could make them rich. Now they are poor—so inexperienced, so stupid, that they have no other hope but him who called them. Jesus knows all about the others too, the representatives and preachers of the national religion, who enjoy greatness and renown, whose feet are firmly planted on the earth, who are deeply rooted in the culture and piety of the people and molded by the spirit of the age. Yet it is not they, but the disciples who are called blessed—theirs is the kingdom of heaven. That kingdom dawns on them, the little band who for the sake of Jesus live a life of absolute renunciation and poverty. And in that very poverty they are heirs of the kingdom. They have their treasure in secret, they find it on the cross. And they have the promise that they will one day visibly enjoy the glory of the kingdom, which in principle is already realized in the utter poverty of the cross.

The experience of transcendence is Jesus' being-for-others. His omnipotence, omniscience, and omnipresence arise solely out of his freedom from self, out of his freedom to be for the others even unto death.

Behind all the slogans and catchwords of ecclesiastical contro-versy, necessary though they are, there arises a more deter-mined quest for him who is the sole object of it all, for Jesus Christ himself. What did Jesus mean to say to us? What is his will for us today? How can he help us to be good Christians in the modern world? In the last resort, what we want to know is not, what would this or that man, or this or that church, have of us, but what Jesus Christ himself wants of us. When we go to church and listen to the sermon, what we want to hear is his word—and that not merely for selfish reasons, but for the sake of the many for whom the church and her message are foreign. We have a strange feeling that if Jesus himself—Jesus alone with his word—could come into our midst at sermon time, we should find quite a different set of men hearing the word, and quite a different set rejecting it.

Community water supply in Berlin-Wedding

Zion Church, Berlin, viewed from the pulpit
from which Dietrich Bonhoeffer preached

Cheap grace is the preaching of forgiveness without requiring repentance, baptism without church discipline, communion without confession, absolution without personal confession. Cheap grace is grace without discipleship, grace without the cross, grace without Jesus Christ, living and incarnate.

Costly grace is the treasure hidden in the field; for the sake of it a man will gladly go and sell all that he has. It is the pearl of great price to buy which the merchant will sell all his goods. It is the kingly rule of Christ, for whose sake a man will pluck out the eye which causes him to stumble, it is the call of Jesus Christ at which the disciple leaves his nets and follows him.

Costly grace is the gospel which must be sought again and again, the gift which must be asked for, the door at which a man must knock.

Such grace is costly because it calls us to follow, and it is grace because it calls us to follow Jesus Christ. It is costly because it costs a man his life, and it is grace because it gives a man the only true life.

Altar of Zion Church

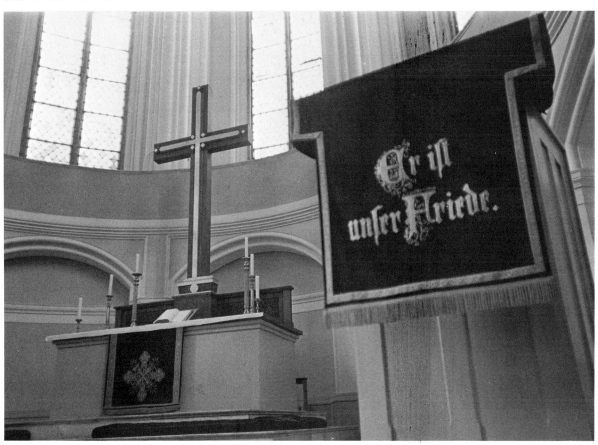

Memorial plaque erected at Zion Church

I hurled myself into my work in an unchristian and unhumble manner.... Then something else came along, something which has permanently changed my life and its direction.... I had often preached, I had seen a lot of the church, I had talked and written about it, but I had not yet become a Christian. (I know that until then I had been using the cause of Jesus Christ to my own advantage.)

The Bible, most particularly the Sermon on the Mount, has freed me from all this. Since then everything has changed.... I now realized that the life of a servant of Jesus Christ must belong to the church, and step by step it became clearer to me to what extent this must be so.

Then came the distress of 1933. That strengthened my conviction. And then too I found others ready to concentrate their attention on this goal. All that mattered to me was the renewal of the church and of the pastoral profession....

Christian pacificism, which I had attacked passionately until shortly before, suddenly revealed itself as a matter of course.... My vocation lies before me. What God will make of it, I do not know....

I believe we shall only perceive the gloriousness of this vocation in the times to come and the events they will bring. If only we can hold out.

Zingsthof on the Baltic, where Bonhoeffer helped to found a clandestine Preachers' Seminary for the Confessing Church in 1935. Within two months the seminary moved to Finkenwalde. Today Zingsthof is used by the Evangelical Church as a summer campground.

"Manor Mount," the parsonage of the Church of St. Paul in Sydenham, London, where Bonhoeffer lived from 1933–35

I believe in the principle of our universal Christian brotherhood which rises above all national interest.

When the Bible speaks of following Jesus, it is proclaiming a discipleship which will liberate mankind from all man-made dogmas, from every burden and oppression, from every anxiety and torture which afflicts the conscience. If they follow Jesus, men escape from the hard yoke of their own laws, and submit to the kindly yoke of Jesus Christ. But does this mean that we ignore the seriousness of his commands? Far from it. We can only achieve perfect liberty and enjoy fellowship with Jesus when his command, his call to absolute discipleship, is appreciated in its entirety. Only the man who follows the command of Jesus single-mindedly, and unresistingly lets his yoke rest upon him, finds his burden easy, and under its gentle pressure receives the power to persevere in the right way.

But one question still troubles us. What can the call to discipleship mean today for the worker, the businessman, the squire, and the soldier? Does it not lead to an intolerable dichotomy between our lives as workers in the world and our lives as Christians? If Christianity means following Christ, is it not a religion for a small minority, a spiritual elite? Does it not mean the repudiation of the great mass of society, and a hearty contempt for the weak and the poor? Yet surely such an attitude is the exact opposite of the gracious mercy of Jesus Christ, who came to the publicans and sinners, the weak and the poor, the erring and the hopeless. Are those who belong to Jesus only a few, or are they many? He died on a cross alone, abandoned by his disciples. With him were crucified, not two of his followers, but two murderers. But they all stood beneath the cross, enemies and believers, doubters and cowards, revilers and devoted followers. His prayer, in that hour, and his forgiveness, was meant for them all, and for all their sins. The mercy and love of God are at work even in the midst of his enemies.

By willing endurance we cause suffering to pass. Evil becomes a spent force when we put up no resistance. By refusing to pay back the enemy in his own coin, and by preferring to suffer without resistance, the Christian exhibits the sinfulness of contumely and insult. Violence stands condemned by its failure to evoke counter-violence. When a man unjustly demands that I should give him my coat, I offer him my cloak also, and so counter his demand; when he requires me to go the other mile, I go willingly, and show up his exploitation of my service for what it is. To leave everything behind at the call of Christ is to be content with him alone, and to follow only him. By his willingly renouncing self-defense, the Christian affirms his absolute adherence to Jesus, and his freedom from the tyranny of his own ego. The exclusiveness of this adherence is the only power which can overcome evil.

Dunes and beach on the Baltic, near Zingsthof, where Bonhoeffer frequently took seminarians for discussions and recreation

The sun is a special favorite of mine and has reminded me often of the fact that man is created from earth and does not consist of air and thoughts. This went so far that once, when I was asked to preach in Cuba at Christmastime, coming from the ice of North America into the blooming vegetation, I almost succumbed to the sun cult and hardly knew what I should have preached. It was a real crisis, and something of this comes over me every summer when I feel the sun. To me the sun is not an astronomical entity, but something like a living power which I love and fear. I find it cowardly to look past these realities rationally. . . . So must patience, joy, gratitude, and calm assert themselves against all sorts of resistance. It says in the psalm, "God is sun and shield." To recognize and experience and believe this is a moment of great grace and by no means an everyday wisdom.

Railroad station used by seminarians at Finkenwalde, near Stettin in Pomerania. *Bruderhaus,* no longer standing, was one kilometer from the station.

28 NOVEMBER 1943

The first Sunday in Advent.—It began with a peaceful night. When I was in bed yesterday evening I looked up for the first time "our" Advent hymns in the Neues Lied. I can hardly hum any of them to myself without being reminded of Finkenwalde, Schlönwitz, and Sigurdshof. Early this morning I held my Sunday service, hung up the Advent wreath on a nail, and fastened Lippi's picture of the Nativity in the middle of it. At breakfast I greatly enjoyed the second of your ostrich eggs.

The individual must realize that his hours of aloneness react upon the community. In his solitude he can sunder and besmirch the fellowship, or he can strengthen and hallow it. Every act of self-control of the Christian is also a service to the fellowship.

On the other hand, there is no sin in thought, word, or deed, no matter how personal or secret, that does not inflict injury upon the whole fellowship. An element of sickness gets into the body; perhaps nobody knows where it comes from or in what member it has lodged, but the body is infected. This is the proper metaphor for the Christian community. We are members of a body, not only when we choose to be, but in our whole existence.

Forest at Finkenwalde, near the site of the clandestine seminary

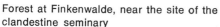

Albrecht Schönherr, one of the first students at Finkenwalde and today a general superintendent of the Evangelical Church in Berlin-Brandenburg, recalls Bonhoeffer's leadership in the Confessing Church which opposed Hitler. "He who deliberately separates himself from the Confessing Church in Germany separates himself from salvation," Bonhoeffer taught in 1936. Schönherr was with his teacher when word came that the government had formed committees to settle the church struggle; Bonhoeffer believed "Church and un-church cannot come to terms." When a person (who later became prominent in the Confessing Church) considered joining the pro-Hitler German church to break it from the inside, Bonhoeffer counseled, "If you board the wrong train, it is no use running along the corridor in the opposite direction."

Many people seek fellowship because they are afraid to be alone. Because they cannot stand loneliness, they are driven to seek the company of other people. There are Christians, too, who cannot endure being alone, who have had some bad experiences with themselves, who hope they will gain some help in association with others. They are generally disappointed. Then they blame the fellowship for what is really their own fault. The Christian community is not a spiritual sanatorium. The person who comes into a fellowship because he is running away from himself is misusing it for the sake of diversion, no matter how spiritual this diversion may appear. He is really not seeking community at all, but only distraction which will allow him to forget his loneliness for a brief time, the very alienation that creates the deadly isolation of man. The disintegration of communication and all genuine experience, and finally resignation and spiritual death, are the result of such attempts to find a cure.

Church in Schlawe, now Slawno, Poland, where curates trained for the Confessing Church after the Preachers' Seminary at Finkenwalde was closed by the Gestapo

Every day brings to the Christian many hours in which he will be alone in an unchristian environment. These are the times of testing. This is the test of true meditation and true Christian community. Has the fellowship served to make the individual free, strong, and mature, or has it made him weak and dependent? Has it taken him by the hand for a while in order that he may learn again to walk by himself, or has it made him uneasy and unsure? This is one of the most searching and critical questions that can be put to any Christian fellowship.

Furthermore, this is the place where we find out whether the Christian's meditation has led him into the unreal, from which he awakens in terror when he returns to the workaday world, or whether it has led him into a real contract with God, from which he emerges strengthened and purified. Has it transported him for a moment into a spiritual ecstasy that vanishes when everyday life returns, or has it lodged the Word of God so securely and deeply in his heart that it holds and fortifies him, impelling him to active love, to obedience, to good works? Only the day can decide.

Country road at Slawno, Poland (formerly Schlawe, Germany)

Oskar Hammelsbeck shared with Dietrich Bonhoeffer the responsibility of training young men to be pastors and future leaders of the Confessing Church. When the so-called Himmler Decree closed the preachers' seminaries and church colleges, Bonhoeffer led his students to an underground school at Finkenwalde and Hammelsbeck camouflaged his "young brethren" as a "team curacy." The two men also worked together on memoranda for the Confessing Church on such subjects as the Jewish question, the liquidation of the mentally deficient, and on church discipline. Bonhoeffer confided to Hammelsbeck that he was involved in the resistance to Hitler, following his conviction that "the structure of responsible action includes both readiness to accept guilt and freedom. . . . If any man tries to escape guilt in responsibility he detaches himself from the ultimate reality of human existence, and what is more he cuts himself off from the redeeming mystery of Christ's bearing guilt without sin and he has no share in the divine justification which lies upon this event."

I have had the time to think and to pray about my situation and that of my nation and to have God's will for me clarified. I have come to the conclusion that I have made a mistake in coming to America. I must live through this difficult period of our national history with the Christian people of Germany. I will have no right to participate in the reconstruction of Christian life in Germany after the war if I do not share the trials of this time with my people. . . . Christians in Germany will face the terrible alternative of either willing the defeat of their nation in order that Christian civilization may survive, or willing the victory of their nation and thereby destroying our civilization. I know which of these alternatives I must choose, but I cannot make that choice in security.

Union Theological Seminary in New York, where Dietrich studied in 1930–31, offered him a haven after the rise of Hitler. After a few weeks there he decided to return and share the struggle with his people.

Professor Reinhold Niebuhr made the arrangements for Dietrich to come to America and was frequently mentioned in the Bonhoeffer papers.

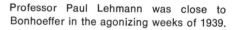

Professor Paul Lehmann was close to Bonhoeffer in the agonizing weeks of 1939.

Let the Christian remain in the world, not because of the good gifts of creation, nor because of his responsibility for the course of the world, but for the sake of the body of the incarnate Christ and for the sake of the church. Let him remain in the world to engage in frontal assault on it, and let him live the life of his secular calling in order to show himself as a stranger in this world all the more. But that is only possible if we are visible members of the church. The antithesis between the world and the church must be borne out in the world. That was the purpose of the incarnation. That is why Christ died among his enemies. That is the reason and the only reason why the slave must remain a slave and the Christian remain subject to the powers that be.

Benedictine Monastery at Ettal, Germany, where Bonhoeffer awaited orders and worked on his *Ethics*

Room used by Bonhoeffer at Monastery Hotel in Ettal

It is true, of course, that what is an unspeakable gift of God for the lonely individual is easily disregarded and trodden underfoot by those who have the gift every day. It is easily forgotten that the fellowship of Christian brethren is a gift of grace, a gift of the kingdom of God that any day may be taken from us, that the time that still separates us from utter loneliness may be brief indeed. Therefore, let him who until now has had the privilege of living a common Christian life with other Christians praise God's grace from the bottom of his heart. Let him thank God on his knees and declare: It is grace, nothing but grace, that we are allowed to live in community with Christian brethren.

. . . . a man takes up his position against the world in the world; the calling is the place at which the call of Christ is answered, the place at which a man lives responsibly. Thus the task which is appointed for me in my calling is a limited one, but at the same time the responsibility to the call of Jesus Christ breaks through all limits.

The misunderstanding on the part of medieval monasticism does not lie in its recognition of the fact that the call of Jesus Christ involves man in a struggle against the world but in its attempt to find a place which is not the world and at which this call can, therefore, be answered more fitly. In this vain endeavor to escape from the world no serious consideration is given either to the "no" of God, which is addressed to the whole world, including the monastery, or to God's "yes," in which he reconciles the world with himself.

Harry Johannsen sits on the steps of his home in Sigtuna, Sweden, where on May 30, 1942, Bonhoeffer paid a secret visit to Bishop G. K. A. Bell of Chichester, England, to describe the plot against Hitler.

If a drunken driver is at the wheel, it is not just the minister's job to comfort the relations of those he has killed, but if possible to seize the steering wheel.

Christians do not wish to escape repentance, or chaos, if it is God's will to bring it upon us. We must take this judgment as Christians.

If any man tries to escape guilt in responsibility he detaches himself from the ultimate reality of human existence, and what is more he cuts himself off from the redeeming mystery of Christ's bearing guilt without sin, and he has no share in the divine justification which lies upon this event. He sets his own personal innocence above his responsibility for men, and he is blind to the more irredeemable guilt which he incurs precisely in this; he is blind also to the fact that real innocence shows it-self precisely in a man's entering into the fellowship of guilt for the sake of other men. . . . From what has just been said it emerges that the structure of responsible action includes both readiness to accept guilt and freedom.

3

Freedom Yielded

SUFFERING

See what a transformation! These hands so active and powerful
Now are tied, and alone and fainting, you see where your work ends.
Yet you are confident still, and gladly commit what is rightful
Into a stronger hand, and say that you are contented.
You were free from a moment of bliss, then you yielded your freedom
Into the hand of God, that he might perfect it in glory.

ven at the time of his arrest, Dietrich Bonhoeffer seemed adequately prepared for all things. There was no pounding at the door in the middle of the night, no capture of the prisoner in a theatrical style. Dietrich seemed in complete control. Months earlier his brother-in-law had learned that the Central Bureau for the Security of the *Reich* was assembling a dossier and was planning his arrest. He had seen other critics of Hitler arrested and he knew what to expect.

Then, one morning in April 1943, Dietrich learned that his sister's husband, Hans von Dohnanyi, had been arrested at his home. So, without panic, almost casually, Dietrich made himself, his family, and even his room as ready as possible. Certain documents, including parts of his unfinished *Ethics*, were hidden in the rafters. Other misleading or unimportant papers were left on the desk. With outward calm the thirty-seven-year-old minister awaited the inevitable black automobile.

Dietrich was taken to the military section of Tegel prison, in Berlin, where he spent a total of eighteen months. He was an unusual prisoner. In the midst of the Allied air raids he ministered to fellow inmates and—one suspects —even to the prison officials. The compassion, the overriding religious insight, and the carefully coded messages in his letters amazed the censors. An extensive correspondence, much of which is preserved in *Letters and Papers from Prison,* was possible because he won the friendship of his warders and because his uncle, General Von Hase, was the commandant of Berlin.

Surely it is no accident that some of history's most significant religious literature has been written in prisons. The apostle Paul, who described himself as a "prisoner for Christ's sake," wrote his letters to the Christians of Philippi and Colossae, and a personal note to Philemon, while he was in Roman chains. In these epistles, and possibly also in the letter to the Ephesians, the apostle looked beyond the walls which surrounded him to the great issues facing the early church. John Bunyan, in another century, began his classic *Pilgrim's Progress* in Bedford gaol. The definitive statement on civil disobedience in the 1960s was the *Letter from the Birmingham City Jail* sent to the clergymen of America by Martin Luther King, Jr. Like these men, and others who were imprisoned for their faithfulness to the gospel, Dietrich Bonhoeffer redeemed the bitter months of confinement by his actions and his words.

One cannot minimize the bitterness of his imprisonment. Especially for gregarious souls like Dietrich, the arrest and subsequent incarceration brought a "violent mental upheaval." Only a few months earlier he had become engaged to Maria von Wedemeyer and his tender letters and references to her reveal the depths of his solitude and isolation. Yet Dietrich took pains to comfort those whose loneliness was compounded by their anxieties for his welfare and future. In his first letter to his parents, written nine days after his arrest, he made light of the discomforts that one generally associates with prison life, the "physical hardships," and even the "hard prison bed." He confessed that "in coming to terms with the new situation" physical things had taken a back seat and that he had found his new life to be an enriching experience. "A good spiritual turkish bath," he called it.

Nevertheless, there was acute anxiety spelled only by his constant study and by his love for Paul Gerhardt's hymns, which he committed to memory. He once described his situation as "perhaps not so very different here from anywhere else. I read, meditate, write, pace up and down my cell —without rubbing myself sore against the walls like a polar bear." His keen sense of humor, which sparkled through his letters, was matched by the sense of discipline and hope which he had learned as a child. "The great thing," he wrote to his parents, "is to stick to what one still has and can do —there is still plenty left—and not to be dominated by the thought of what one cannot do, and by feelings of resentment and discontent."

Through brief visits and notes from Maria, his close friend Eberhard Bethge, and his parents, Dietrich was kept informed about the people who meant so much to him and the cause for which he had yielded his freedom. When Bethge was married, Dietrich sent him a wedding sermon which he had written in his cell. A baptismal letter greeted their first child. Frequently he expressed concern for his parents' safety during the air raids and for his brother-in-law and for Martin Niemöller, who also had been arrested.

The turning point came when word reached Dietrich that the attempt to assassinate Hitler on July 20, 1944, had failed. Sensing then what would surely happen to him, he wrote a brief letter to Bethge and sent a poem, "Stations on the Road to Freedom," with its poignantly autobiographical overtones. With the failure of the coup, which had been so carefully planned, he felt the impact of his imprisonment acutely. He felt absolutely alone, and his work seemed at an end. Yet he was ready to put his trust in a stronger hand, in the hand of God.

Thereafter he was guarded with greater care and, since it might implicate others, he was even more cautious with his correspondence. When the Zossen documents helped the Gestapo to identify members of the resistance movement in September, Dietrich was moved to solitary confinement at the prison on Prinz Albrecht Strasse.

With great courage, he communicated with Fabian von Schlabrendorff, Maria's cousin, who was assigned a neighboring cell in the Gestapo prison. Like Dietrich, Von Schlabrendorff had been involved in the resistance, and he endured the brutal torture which the young minister described with a single word: disgusting.

Von Schlabrendorff felt that Dietrich's "noble and pure soul must have suffered deeply. But he betrayed no sign of it. He was always good-tempered, always of the same kindliness and politeness toward everybody. . . . He always

cheered me up and comforted me. He never tired of repeating that the only fight which is lost is that which we give up."

The two were standing together in the bomb shelter on February 3, 1945, when an air raid turned the city of Berlin into a pile of rubble and the Gestapo headquarters into an inferno. Von Schlabrendorff remembers how an enormous explosion rocked the prison "like a ship tossing in the storm." At that moment, Dietrich Bonhoeffer showed his mettle. Standing calm, motionless, and relaxed, he acted as if nothing had happened. This helped the other prisoners to maintain their equilibrium.

Four days later, Bonhoeffer and a group of inmates were taken from Prinz Albrecht Strasse to Buchenwald and from there to a concentration camp in Regensburg. On April 5 they were transported to a detention center at Schönberg.

While Dietrich, as part of the Resistance Group, was working to meet with the Allies, German troops had overrun Denmark, Norway, Belgium, Holland, and France, London had been devastated, and the bitter battle at Stalingrad had stopped the eastward thrust of the German armies.

German troops entering Paris, July 1940

St. Paul's Cathedral surrounded by the devastation of London after German bombings, May 1941

The German war machine was fatally weakened at Stalingrad, December 1942.

German troops completely defeated at Stalingrad plod wearily to Russian prison camps, January 1943.

U.S. troops advancing at Salerno. By the time that American troops were driving northward through Italy, Dietrich was already in prison, October 1943.

Allied troops landing at Normandy in June 1944

Jesus Christ lived in the midst of his enemies. At the end all his disciples deserted him. On the cross he was utterly alone, surrounded by evildoers and mockers. For this cause he had come, to bring peace to the enemies of God. So the Christian, too, belongs not in the seclusion of a cloistered life but in the thick of foes. There is his commission, his work. "The kingdom is to be in the midst of your enemies. And he who will not suffer this does not want to be of the kingdom of Christ; he wants to be among friends, to sit among roses and lilies, not with the bad people but the devout people. O you blasphemers and betrayers of Christ! If Christ had done what you are doing who would ever have been spared?" (Luther)

Room at Marienburger Allee 43 in which Dietrich Bonhoeffer was arrested on April 5, 1943

There is hardly one of us who has not known what it is to be betrayed. The figure of Judas, which we used to find so difficult to understand, is now fairly familiar to us. The air that we breathe is so polluted by mistrust that it almost chokes us. But where we have broken through the layer of mistrust, we have been able to discover a confidence hitherto undreamed of. Where we trust, we have learnt to put our very lives into the hands of others; in the face of all the different interpretations that have been put on our lives and actions, we have learnt to trust unreservedly. We now know that only such confidence, which is always a venture, though a glad and positive venture, enables us really to live and work. We know that it is most reprehensible to sow and encourage mistrust, and that our duty is rather to foster and strengthen confidence wherever we can. Trust will always be one of the greatest, rarest, and happiest blessings of our life in community, though it can emerge only on the dark background of a necessary mistrust. We have learnt never to trust a scoundrel an inch, but to give ourselves to the trustworthy without reserve.

The homes of men are not, like the shelters of animals, merely the means of protection against bad weather and the night or merely places for rearing the young; they are places in which a man may relish the joys of his personal life in the intimacy and security of his family and of his property. Eating and drinking do not merely serve the purpose of keeping the body in good health, but they afford natural joy in bodily living. Clothing is not intended merely as a mean covering for the body, but also as an adornment of the body. Recreation is not designed solely to increase working efficiency, but it provides the body with its due measure of repose and enjoyment. Play is by its nature remote from all subordination to purpose, and it thus demonstrates most clearly that the life of the body is an end in itself. Sex is not only the means of reproduction, but, independently of this defined purpose, it brings with it its own joy, in married life, in the love of two human beings for one another. From all this it emerges that the meaning of bodily life never lies solely in its subordination to its final purpose. The life of the body assumes its full significance only with the fulfillment of its inherent claim to joy.

The house at Marienburger Allee 43 where the Gestapo arrested Bonhoeffer and his two sisters and their husbands. The home is now a student center.

The table fellowship of Christians implies obligation. It is our daily bread that we eat, not my own. We share our bread. Thus we are firmly bound to one another not only in the Spirit but in our whole physical being. The one bread that is given to our fellowship links us together in a firm covenant. Now none dares go hungry as long as another has bread, and he who breaks this fellowship of the physical life also breaks the fellowship of the Spirit.

When we are called to follow Christ, we are summoned to an exclusive attachment to his person. The grace of his call bursts all the bonds of legalism. It is a gracious call, a gracious commandment. It transcends the difference between the law and the gospel. Christ calls, the disciple follows; that is grace and commandment in one. "I will walk at liberty: for I seek thy commandments" (Ps. 119:45).

One may ask whether there have ever before in human history been people with so little ground under their feet—people to whom every available alternative seemed equally intolerable, repugnant, and futile, who looked beyond all these existing alternatives for the source of their strength so entirely in the past or in the future, and who yet, without being dreamers, were able to await the success of their cause so quietly and confidently. Or perhaps one should rather ask whether the responsible thinking people of any generation that stood at a turning point in history did not feel much as we do, simply because something new was emerging that could not be seen in the existing alternatives.

Exercise yard at Tegel Prison in Berlin

It looks as if something will be decided about me in a week's time. I hope it will. If it turns out that they send me in Martin's * direction (though I don't think that is likely), please make your mind easy about it. I am really not at all worried as to what happens to me personally. So please don't you worry either.

* Martin Niemöller, who was interned at the concentration camp at Dachau.

Window of Bonhoeffer's cell at Tegel

Cell number 10, to which Bonhoeffer was transferred from the top floor when air raids of Berlin became frequent

Well, you had a rough passage last night. I was very relieved when the captain sent word to me that you were all right. My cell is high up, and the window is kept wide open during alerts, so one has a very clear view of the ghastly firework display on the south side of the city; and without the least feeling of anxiety for myself, I do feel most strongly at such times how utterly absurd it is for me to be kept waiting here doing nothing. I thought the Brüdergemeinde *text for this morning [August 24, 1943] was most appropriate: "And I will give peace in the land, and you shall lie down, and none shall make you afraid" (Lev. 26:6).*

I believe that God can and will bring good out of evil, even out of the greatest evil. For that purpose he needs men who make the best use of everything. I believe that God will give us all the strength we need to help us to resist in all time of distress. But he never gives it in advance, lest we should rely on ourselves and not on him alone. A faith such as this should allay all our fears for the future. I believe that even our mistakes and shortcomings are turned to good account, and that it is no harder for God to deal with them than with our supposedly good deeds. I believe that God is no timeless fate, but that he waits for and answers sincere prayers and responsible actions.

View from Bonhoeffer's cell, across the exercise yard

I often wonder who I really am—the man who goes on squirming under these ghastly experiences in wretchedness that cries to heaven, or the man who scourges himself and pretends to others (and even to himself) that he is placid, cheerful, composed, and in control of himself, and allows people to admire him for it (i.e., for playing the part—or is it not playing a part?). What does one's attitude mean, anyway? In short, I know less than ever about myself, and I am no longer attaching any importance to it. I have had more than enough psychology, and I am less and less inclined to analyze the state of my soul. That is why I value Stifter and Gotthelf so much. There is something more at stake than self-knowledge. . . .

I sometimes feel as if my life were more or less over, and as if all I had to do now were to finish my Ethics. *But, you know, when I feel like this, there comes over me a longing (unlike any other that I experience) not to vanish without a trace—an Old Testament rather than a New Testament wish, I suppose . . .*

A prison cell, in which one waits, hopes, does various unessential things, and is completely dependent on the fact that the door of freedom has to be opened from the outside, is not a bad picture of Advent.

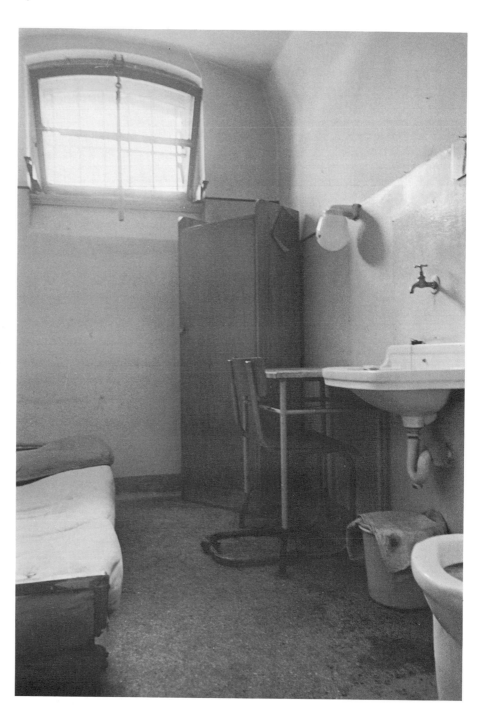

It is infinitely easier to suffer in obedience to a human command than in the freedom of one's own responsibility. It is infinitely easier to suffer with others than to suffer alone. It is infinitely easier to suffer publicly and honorably than apart and ignominiously. It is infinitely easier to suffer through staking one's life than to suffer spiritually. Christ suffered as a free man alone, apart and in ignominy, in body and spirit; and since then many Christians have suffered with him.

The "as though it were a part of me" * is perfectly true, as I have often felt after hearing that one of my colleagues or pupils had been killed. I think it is a literal fact of nature that human life extends far beyond our physical existence. Probably a mother feels this more strongly than anyone else. There are two passages in the Bible which always seem to me to sum the thing up. One is from Jeremiah 45: "Behold, what I have built I am breaking down, and what I have planted I am plucking up. . . . And do you seek great things for yourself? Seek them not . . . but I will give your life as a prize of war . . ."; and the other is from Psalm 60: "Thou hast made the land to quake, thou hast rent it open; repair its breaches, for it totters."

I wish you would let me know whether you have had the anti-shrapnel trench dug, and whether it would not be possible for you to have an exit made from the cellar to the trench. That is what Captain M.† has done. . . .

I am still getting on all right. I have been moved two floors lower because of the raids, and now it is very nice to have a direct view from my window onto the church towers.

---

* *"Als wär's ein Stück von mir"* from the soldier's song, *"Ich hatt' einen Kameraden."*

† Captain Maetz, the commandant of the military prison in Tegel.

The family home on Wangenheim Strasse
still shows the damage caused by bombing
in 1944–45.

Eberhard Bethge, to whom many of Bonhoeffer's letters from prison were addressed, has devoted his life to preserving his friend's papers.

We had another very lively time last night [March 24, 1944]. The view from the roof here over the city was staggering. I have heard nothing yet about the family. Thank God my parents went to P.* yesterday; but there was not much doing in the West. It seems to me absurd how one cannot help hoping, when an air raid is announced, that it will be the turn of other places this time—as the saying goes, "Holy St. Florian, spare my house, set others on fire"—wanting to push off onto others what one fears for oneself: "Perhaps they will get no further than Magdeburg or Stettin this time"; how often have I heard that fervent wish expressed! Such moments make one very conscious of natura corrupta *and* peccatum originale, *and to that extent they may be quite salutary. Incidentally, there has been a very marked increase in air activity during the last few days, and it makes one wonder whether it is not a substitute for the invasion that is not materializing.*

* Pätzig in Neumark, an estate belonging to the parents of Maria von Wedemeyer.

Marriage is more than your love for each other. It has a higher dignity and power, for it is God's holy ordinance, through which he wills to perpetuate the human race till the end of time. In your love you see only your two selves in the world, but in marriage you are a link in the chain of the generations, which God causes to come and to pass away to his glory, and calls into his kingdom. In your love you see only the heaven of your happiness, but in marriage you are placed at a post of responsibility toward the world and mankind. Your love is your own private possession, but marriage is more than something personal—it is a status, an office. Just as it is the crown, and not merely the will to rule, that makes the king, so it is marriage, and not merely your love for each other, that joins you together in the sight of God and man. . . . It is not your love that sustains the marriage, but from now on, the marriage that sustains your love.

Renate Schleicher and Eberhard Bethge were to have been married by Dietrich Bonhoeffer. From his prison cell at Tegel, the young German pastor sent a wedding sermon.

PRAYERS FOR FELLOW-PRISONERS

[Composed for Christmas 1943 at the suggestion of Harald Poelchau, prison chaplain at Tegel]

O God, early in the morning I cry to thee.
Help me to pray
And to concentrate my thoughts on thee;
I cannot do this alone.

In me there is darkness,
But with thee there is light;
I am lonely, but thou leavest me not;
I am feeble in heart, but with thee there is help;
I am restless, but with thee there is patience;
I do not understand thy ways,
But thou knowest the way for me.

. . . .

Lord Jesus Christ,
Thou wast poor
and in distress, a captive and forsaken as I am.
Thou knowest all man's troubles;
Thou abidest with me
when all men fail me;
Thou rememberest and seekest me;
It is thy will that I should know thee
and turn to thee.
Lord, I hear thy call and follow;
Do thou help me.

Harald Poelchau, prison chaplain at Tegel

It would be better if I succeeded in writing to you out of my gratitude, my joy, and my happiness in having you and in keeping the pressure and the impatience of this long imprisonment out of sight. But that would not be truthful, and it would appear to me as an injustice to you. You must know how I really feel and must not take me for a stone saint. . . . I can't very well imagine that you would want to marry one in the first place— and I would also advise against it from my knowledge of church history.

Your life would have been quite different, easier, clearer, simpler had not our path crossed a year ago. But there are only short moments when this thought bothers me. I believe that not only I, but you too, had arrived at the moment in life when we had to meet; neither of us basically has any desire for an easy life, much as we may enjoy beautiful and happy hours in this life, and much as we may have a great longing for these hours today. I believe that happiness lies for both of us at a different and hidden place which is incomprehensible to many. Actually both of us look for challenges (Aufgaben), up to now each for himself, but from now on together. Only in this work will we grow completely together when God gives us the time for it.

Stifter once said, "Pain is a holy angel, who shows treasures to men which otherwise remain forever hidden; through him men have become greater than through all joys of the world." It must be so and I tell this to myself in my present position over and over again—the pain of longing which often can be felt even physically, must be there, and we shall not and need not talk it away. But it needs to be overcome every time, and thus there is an even holier angel than the one of pain, that is the one of joy in God.

Copy of the photograph of Maria von Wedemeyer, taken in 1942, which Bonhoeffer carried with him.

Maria von Wedemeyer-Weller was Bonhoeffer's fiancee at the time of his imprisonment and death. Mrs. Von Wedemeyer-Weller now lives near Boston.

88

Emmi Bonhoeffer, whose husband Klaus was murdered by the Gestapo in 1945 for his opposition to Hitler, recalls how much her brother-in-law loved flowers. To his parents he wrote from prison on October 13, 1943:

I have in front of me the gay bunch of dahlias that you brought me yesterday; it reminds me of the lovely hour that I was able to have with you, and of the garden, and in general of how beautiful the world can be in these autumn days. One of Storm's verses that I came across the other day just about expresses this mood, and keeps going through my head like a tune that one cannot get rid of:

> Und geht es draussen noch so toll,
>   unchristlich oder christlich,
> ist doch die Welt, die schöne Welt
> so gänzlich unverwüstlich.*

All that is needed to bring that home to one is a few gay autumn flowers, the view from the cell window, and half an hour's "exercise" in the prison yard, where there are, in fact, a few beautiful chestnut and lime trees. But in the last resort, for me at any rate, the "world" consists of a few people whom I should like to see and to be with. . . . If, besides that, I could sometimes hear a good sermon on Sundays—I sometimes hear fragments of the chorales that are carried along by the breeze—it would be still better . . .

* And however crazy, or Christian,
    or unchristian things may be out-
        side,
  this world, this beautiful world
  is quite indestructible.

Emmi Bonhoeffer, Dietrich's sister-in-law,
in her garden at Frankfurt am Main

4

The Way to Freedom Eternal

DEATH

Come now, highest of feasts on the way to freedom eternal,
Death, strike off the fetters, break down the walls that oppress us,
Our bedazzled soul and our ephemeral body,
That we may see at last the sight which here was not vouchsafed us.
Freedom, we sought you long in discipline, action, suffering.
Now as we die we see you and know you at last, face to face.

he end seemed imminent for Germany, for its mad *Führer,* and for the band of men who risked their lives to save Germany by removing the dictator.

As Allied aircraft continued to pound Berlin relentlessly, the military machine which had once goose-stepped across Europe began to crumble. The General Staff was losing heart; only Adolf Hitler stood firm in the face of heavy Russian pressure in the East and increasing Allied momentum in the West.

In what must have been an act of desperation, the orders were given that some men who had been involved in the resistance movement, especially in the putsch of July 20, were to be transferred from various prisons to the extermination camp at Flossenbürg.

Among the distinguished occupants of the windowless cellar in Buchenwald was Wassili Kokorin, nephew of Molotov, a pair of German generals who had defied their leader, a former secretary of state, and the activist theologian Dietrich Bonhoeffer. These men were herded into a primitive truck and driven by a circuitous route to a town prison in Regensburg. The jail was already crowded with the families of prominent resistance leaders and well-known enemy prisoners. An English airman in the group was impressed by the way the new arrivals greeted their friends, sharing news as at a great reception, even if the information was tragic and distasteful.

Again on the road in the ancient vehicle, Bonhoeffer carried three precious possessions: his Bible, a volume of Plutarch, and a copy of Goethe. When the truck broke down the men were transferred to a bus whose driver told friendly village girls that his passengers were going to make an important propaganda film. Finally, in mid-afternoon, the prisoners reached the pleasant valley of Schönberg and were taken to the school where the "special cases" already were detained.

Bonhoeffer sat for a long time at an open window, enjoying the warm spring air of that Good Friday afternoon. He learned a few words of Russian from Kokorin and told him the nature of the Christian belief. Relieved to be away from enemy action and feeling less like prisoners, Bonhoeffer, Kokorin, and Secretary of State Pünder wrote their names over the beds which had been made up with clean linens and brightly colored blankets.

For a week the easy banter continued. There were lessons in Russian, talk of an early Allied victory, bathing in the bright sun. Elsewhere, however, the still-efficient machinery of the Secret Service ground on. In the concentration camp at Sachsenhausen Dietrich's brother-in-law Von Dohnanyi was summarily court-martialed and condemned to death. After a meeting with Hitler himself, a high-ranking official drove to Flossenbürg carrying the important files and the candid diary of Admiral Canaris, leader of the abortive coup.

But when the court-martial was ready, Bonhoeffer was missing. Guards challenged other prisoners, believing that the preacher was masquerading. Then, despite the disarray of the military and civilian government, he was found in Schönberg on Sunday, April 8.

Pünder had suggested that Dietrich conduct a morning service, but the sensitive pastor was reluctant. Most of the prisoners were Roman Catholics and he was not eager to embarrass his new friend Kokorin, whom he hoped to visit in Moscow. But the Russian urged him on, and Dietrich Bonhoeffer yielded to the general wish. His texts were from Isaiah and 1 Peter: "And with his stripes we are healed" and "By his great mercy we have been born anew to a living hope through the resurrection of Jesus." He spoke simply but movingly of the thoughts and prayers of all the prisoners.

Scarcely had he finished when two civilian guards entered. "Prisoner Bonhoeffer, get ready to come with us."

He had time to say a few farewells. He wrote his name in three places in the book of Plutarch and left it as a reminder of his short stay in Schönberg. Via the English airman he sent farewell greetings to the Bishop of Chichester. "This is the end, for me the beginning of life."

Late in the evening Bonhoeffer met his accusers and the others who had shared in the plot. In the grey dawn of April 9, Bonhoeffer, Canaris, Oster, Sack, Strünk, and Gehre were hanged.

After the February 3, 1945 bombing of
Berlin by Allied planes, Dietrich's parents
sent him a letter saying, "We shall remain
in Berlin." This was their last communication with Dietrich.

Berlin in ruins, May 1945

First American photo of Russians in Berlin,
June 1945

Ruins of the Protestant cathedral, Berlin,
1945

Among Bonhoeffer's fellow-prisoners at Schönberg was an English officer, Payne Best, who recorded his final sermon:

Bonhoeffer . . . was all humility and sweetness; he always seemed to me to diffuse an atmosphere of happiness, of joy in every smallest event in life, and of deep gratitude for the mere fact that he was alive. . . . He was one of the very few men that I have ever met to whom God was real and close. . . . The following day, Sunday 8th April, 1945, Pastor Bonhoeffer held a little service and spoke to us in a manner which reached the hearts of all, finding just the right words to express the spirit of our imprisonment and the thoughts and resolutions which it brought. He had hardly finished his last prayer when the door opened and two evil-looking men in civilian clothes came in and said: "Prisoner Bonhoeffer, get ready to come with us." Those words "come with us"—for all prisoners they had come to mean one thing only—the scaffold.

We bade him good-bye—he drew me aside—"This is the end," he said. "For me the beginning of life," and then he gave a message to give, if I could, to the Bishop of Chichester. . . . Next day, at Flossenbürg, he was hanged.

Quoted by Eberhard Bethge

Schoolhouse in Schönberg where Bonhoeffer and other "important prisoners" were
held near the end of the war

Countryside between Schönberg and Flossenbürg, to which Bonhoeffer was moved for court-martial and execution

What, then, is joy? What, then, is sorrow?
Time alone can decide between them,
when the immediate poignant happening
lengthens out to continuous wearisome suffering,
when the labored creeping moments of daylight
slowly uncover the fullness of our disaster,
sorrow's unmistakable features.

Then do most of our kind,
sated, if only by the monotony
of unrelieved unhappiness,
turn away from the drama, disillusioned,
uncompassionate.

O ye mothers and loved ones—then, ah, then
comes your hour, the hour for true devotion.
Then your hour comes, ye friends and brothers!
Loyal hearts can change the face of sorrow,
softly encircle it with love's most gentle
unearthly radiance.

Ruin of detention house at Flossenbürg

Detention area at Flossenbürg

Cell at Flossenbürg

Fabian von Schlabrendorff, a fellow-prisoner of the Gestapo at Prinz Albrecht Strasse, had participated in an attempt to assassinate Hitler. A cousin of Maria von Wedemeyer, to whom Bonhoeffer was engaged, Von Schlabrendorff recalls how Bonhoeffer encouraged him during periods of depression. "He always cheered me up and comforted me," the Wiesbaden lawyer has written. "He never tired of repeating that the only fight which is lost is that which we give up." Toward the end of the war, Von Schlabrendorff was taken to the extermination camp at Flossenbürg. Twice during the night of April 7, 1945, he was awakened by the warders and accused of being Bonhoeffer. Three days later he learned that Bonhoeffer had been located at Schönberg, brought to Flossenbürg, and hanged on the direct orders of Himmler.

Fabian von Schlabrendorff

Only he who believes is obedient, and only he who is obedient believes.

It is quite unbiblical to hold the first proposition without the second. We think we understand when we hear that obedience is possible only where there is faith. Does not obedience follow faith as good fruit grows on a good tree? First, faith, then obedience. If by that we mean that it is faith which justifies, and not the act of obedience, all well and good, for that is the essential and unexceptionable presupposition of all that follows. If however we make a chronological distinction between faith and obedience, and make obedience subsequent to faith, we are divorcing the one from the other—and then we get the practical question, when must obedience begin? Obedience remains separated from faith. From the point of view of justification it is necessary thus to separate them, but we must never lose sight of their essential unity. For faith is only real when there is obedience, never without it, and faith only becomes faith in the act of obedience.

Laundry at Flossenbürg, used for Bonhoeffer's trial

When Christ calls a man, he bids him come and die.

Flossenbürg

To a fellow-prisoner at Flossenbürg, the English officer Captain
Payne Best, Dietrich Bonhoeffer
whispered, "This is the end, for
me the beginning of life."

Der die Sünde straft und gern vergibt,
Gott, ich habe dieses Volk geliebt.
Dass ich seine Schmach und Lasten trug
und sein Heil geschaut—das ist genug.
Halte, fasse mich! Mir sinkt der Stab,
treuer Gott, bereite mir mein Grab.

God, who dost punish sin and willingly forgive,
I have loved this people.
That I have borne its shame and burdens,
and seen its salvation—that is enough.
Seize me and hold me! My staff is sinking;
O faithful God, prepare my grave.

Steps to execution area

The incognito of his death in the extermination camp at Flossenbürg was so complete that only after long months of anxiety was his family able to obtain information as to when and where it took place. For the executioners, their victim had no name other than the label "Enemy of the State." Thus he was "extinguished," as the officials of that time expressed it, nameless like millions of Jews, his ashes thrown into the wind. There was no funeral, no sermon. And today there is no grave where reverence can make up for what was denied at the time of chaos.

—Eberhard Bethge

Flossenbürg

Hillside near Flossenbürg

Death is the supreme festival on the road to freedom.

Dietrich-Bonhoeffer-Haus in Schönberg

A Postscript

O ye mothers and loved ones—then, ah, then comes your hour, the hour for true devotion. Then your hour comes, ye friends and brothers! Loyal hearts can change the face of sorrow, softly encircle it with love's most gentle unearthly radiance.

Schönberg

Student chapel in Schönberg

A Teachers' Training College has been built in Wuppertal on a street now called Dietrich-Bonhoeffer-Weg. The relief sculpture, modeled by Bonhoeffer's twin sister Sabine Leibholz, was presented by the Minister of Education for North Rhine-Westphalia. Hanging beside it is a reproduction of his poem "Stations on the Way to Freedom," given by the Student Christian Movement.

Foyer at Teachers' College, Wuppertal, West Germany

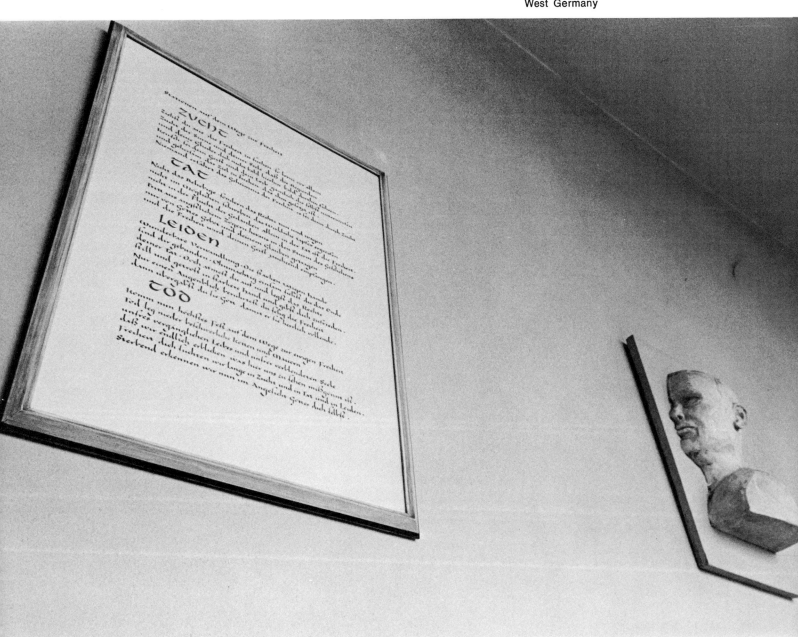

Street in Wuppertal

Holy Trinity Church, London, where a memorial service was held

Chapel of Dietrich Bonhoeffer Church,
London

Bible in Bonhoeffer Church, London, was sent by Dietrich from prison to Bishop Bell of Chichester

126

Dietrich Bonhoeffer Church, Sydenham, London

Acknowledgments

World Council of Churches.

Pages 7-11 — "Not only in Germany . . ." "Dietrich Bonhoeffer, 1945-1965" by W. A. Visser 't Hooft. *The Ecumenical Review,* Vol. XVIII, July 1965, No. 3, pp. 224-31.

Harper & Row, Publishers:

Bonhoeffer, Dietrich. *The Way to Freedom.* New York, 1966. By permission of Harper & Row, Publishers.
Page 58—"I have had time to think . . ."

I Knew Dietrich Bonhoeffer, edited by Wolf-Dieter Zimmermann and Ronald Gregor Smith. Copyright © 1966 in the English translation by Wm. Collins Sons & Co., Ltd., London, and Harper & Row, Publishers, Incorporated, New York. By permission of Harper & Row, Publishers.
Page 5—"He stands for all . . ."
Page 27—"That is not just my bread . . ."
Page 32—"What is a sacrament . . ."
Page 45—"Stony desert of the city . . ."
Page 50—"I believe in the principle . . ."
Page 54—"He who deliberately separates . . ."
Page 54—"Church and un-church . . ."
Page 54—"If you board the wrong train . . ."
Page 57—"The structure of responsible action . . ."
Page 61—"If a drunken driver . . ."
Page 61—"Christians do not wish . . ."
Page 105—"He always cheered me up . . ."
Page 105—"He never tired . . ."
Page 110—"This is the end . . ."

Life Together by Dietrich Bonhoeffer. Copyright 1954 by Harper & Row, Publishers, Incorporated. By permission of the publishers.
Page 32—"The day of the Lord's Supper . . ."
Page 53—"The individual must realize . . ."
Page 55—"Many people seek fellowship . . ."
Page 56—"Every day brings . . ."
Page 60—"It is true . . ."
Page 69—"Jesus Christ lived . . ."
Page 72—"The table fellowship of Christians . . ."

The Macmillan Company:

Bonhoeffer, Dietrich. *The Cost of Discipleship.* New York, 1963. Reprinted with permission of The Macmillan Company from *The Cost of Discipleship* by Dietrich Bonhoeffer. © S.C.M. Press, Ltd. 1959.
Page 36—"It is becoming clearer . . ."
Page 46—"Privation is the lot . . ."
Page 47—"Behind all the slogans . . ."
Page 48—"Cheap grace is the preaching of forgiveness . . ."
Page 50—"When the Bible speaks . . ."
Page 51—"But one question still troubles us. . . ."
Page 51—"By willing endurance . . ."
Page 59—"Let the Christian remain . . ."
Page 72—"When we are called . . ."
Page 106—"Only he who believes . . ."
Page 108—"When Christ calls . . ."

———. *Ethics,* Eberhard Bethge, ed. New York, 1965. Reprinted with permission of The Macmillan Company from *Ethics* by Dietrich Bonhoeffer. © S.C.M. Press, Ltd. 1955.
Page 23—"If you set out . . ."
Page 30—"Conscience comes . . ."
Page 37—"Do and dare . . ."
Page 60—"A man takes up his position . . ."
Page 62—"If any man tries to escape . . ."
Page 63—"See what a transformation! . . ."
Page 71—"The homes of men . . ."
Page 91—"Come now, highest of feasts . . ."

———.*Letters and Papers from Prison.* Eberhard Bethge, ed. Revised edition; New York, 1967. Reprinted with permission of The Macmillan Company from *Letters and Papers from Prison* by Dietrich Bonhoeffer. Copyright 1953 by The Macmillan Company. © S.C.M. Press, Ltd. 1967.
Page 28—"You are the first . . ."
Page 35—"What a blessing . . ."
Page 53—"The first Sunday in Advent . . ."
Page 70—"There is hardly one . . ."
Page 72—"One may ask . . ."
Page 74—"It looks as if . . ."
Page 75—"Well, you had a rough passage . . ."
Page 76—"I believe that God can . . ."
Page 77—"I often wonder . . ."
Page 79—"It is infinitely easier . . . "
Page 79—"The 'as though it were' . . ."
Page 82—"We had another very lively time . . ."
Page 83—"Marriage is more than your love . . ."
Page 84—"O God, early in the morning . . ."
Page 88—"I have in front of me . . ."
Page 96—"Bonhoeffer . . . was all humility . . ."
Page 99—"What, then, is joy? . . ."
Page 110—"*Der die Sünde straft . . .*"
Page 110—"God, who dost punish sin . . ."
Page 114—"Death is the supreme festival . . ."
Page 117—"O ye mothers . . ."

Van Buren, Paul M. *The Secular Meaning of the Gospel.* New York, 1963. Used by permission of The Macmillan Company.
Page 46—"Honesty demands . . ."
Page 46—"The experience of transcendence . . ."

The editors of *Union Seminary Quarterly Review*, Maria von Wedemeyer-Weller, and Eberhard Bethge:

Bethge, Eberhard, "Turning Points in Bonhoeffer's Life and Thought." *Union Seminary Quarterly Re-*

view, XXIII, 1 (Fall 1967), 3-21.

Page 49—"I hurled myself . . ."

Page 112—"The incognito of his death . . ."

Von Wedemeyer-Weller, Maria, "The Other Letters from Prison." *Union Seminary Quarterly Review,* XXIII, 1 (Fall 1967), 23-29.

Page 28—"It happens to be . . ."

Page 52—"The sun is a special favorite . . ."

Page 78—"A prison cell . . ."

Page 86—"It would be better . . ."

Page 86—"Your life would have been . . ."

Page 86—"Stifter once said . . ."

PHOTO CREDITS: Wide World, pages 2, 40 (L), 41 (top L, center R, bottom L), 42, 44, 67, 68 (top, 2d, 3d), 94, 95 (top); Keystone Press, pages 40 (R), 41 (top R, bottom R), 43 (center L, center R); Religious News Service, pages 43 (top L), 95 (bottom); Associated Press, pages 43 (bottom L), 68 (bottom).